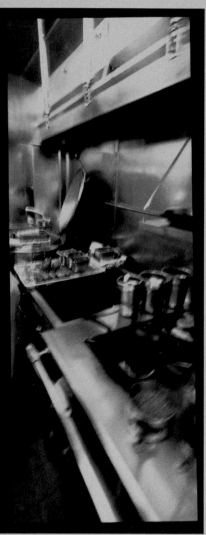

WORKIN'
MORE
KITCHEN
SESSIONS
WITH
CHARLIE
TROTTER

WORKIN' MORE KITCHEN SESSIONS WITH CHARLIE TROTTER

RECIPES BY
CHARLIE TROTTER
AND
SARI ZERNICH

WINE NOTES BY
JASON SMITH

LOCATION PHOTOGRAPHY BY
PAUL ELLEDGE

FOOD PHOTOGRAPHY BY
KIPLING SWEHLA

FOREWORD BY ROCHELLE SMITH

TEN SPEED PRESS
Berkeley | Toronto

Contents

The Making of Charlie Trotter's
15th Anniversary

Workin' more . . . what a concept! When I think about the brilliance that Chef Charlie Trotter (or Charles, as I like to call him) applies to everything culinary, I cannot envision how one could possibly work MORE.

Workin' More Kitchen Sessions with Charlie Trotter is like an album where each song is a hit! It flows sensually, with the ingredients serving as the chef's instruments and the resulting delicacy as the final composition.

The book's companion television series, *Kitchen Sessions,* is incredibly special to me, as I know it is to Chef Trotter. The first episode begins with a celebration of the fifteenth anniversary of Charlie Trotter's restaurant, a celebration that centered on bringing the master of cuisine, Chef Frédy Girardet, out of retirement to prepare a culinary explosion for guests in Chicago. How did this monumental event come about?

Workin' more . . . amazing ideas! While planning a trip to Milan, Italy, for the Marchesi Awards, Charles and I began to brainstorm about ways to make the fifteenth anniversary truly remarkable. We discussed potential sponsors and chefs, and the guest list. Then the ultimate idea occurred to us: convince Chef Girardet to come out of retirement to participate in this once in a lifetime event.

To make that happen, Chef Trotter's mind began workin' more. . . . We knew we had to make this offer to Chef Girardet in person, so we planned a stopover in Geneva, Switzerland, on the way to Milan. Only one problem: Chef Trotter doesn't speak French (except when it comes to food). That's where I came in. I speak French, so I was duly elected to join him on the pilgrimage to make this offer to Chef Girardet.

Off to Switzerland we went . . . workin' on our story to convince Chef Girardet to accept the offer. In case you don't know, Chef Girardet is Charles's hero. Aside from the birth of his wonderful son, Dylan, one of the most memorable moments in Chef Trotter's life was a surprise fortieth birthday dinner prepared by Chef Girardet in his home. Some of Charles's best friends attended the celebration, including Norman Van Aken, Todd English, Larry Stone, Dr. Lee Smith, Steve Greystone, and of course Steven McMillan, whose generosity and vision made the evening extraordinary. So you see, having Chef Girardet at the fifteenth anniversary would be a life-altering moment for Chef Trotter.

We met with Chef Girardet and his assistant, Francesco, for dinner upon our arrival in Switzerland. Initially Chef Girardet was hesitant, but by the end of the dinner the deal was set. Chef Girardet was so excited he even began to discuss what dishes he might prepare.

Fast forward to the trip to pick up Chef Girardet and his team. Only one word can describe the experience: UNBELIEVABLE! This time the adventure crew consisted of Chef Trotter, myself, and master sommelier Larry Stone.

What an amazing adventure that was! Workin' more . . . ideas to ensure Chef Girardet's comfort on the flight from Geneva to Chicago. The airplane cabin was converted into a miniature Trotter's restaurant. We served the Girardet team incredible food, including truffles, caviar, and scallops. The wines poured would make any connoisseur cry. I recall the 1966 Musigny Comte de Vogüé the most, as it was the one I decanted because Larry had fallen asleep. If smiles were priced, then the one on the face of Chef Girardet would have garnered a million dollars!

Chef Girardet was like a kid in a candy store upon arrival in Chicago. He refused to go rest, and instead went directly to the restaurant kitchen and began to view the ingredients for his meal. He even made test soufflés and actually walked them upstairs to ensure they would remain intact on the night they were to be served. What an excellentist (a Trotter-coined phrase).

Workin' more . . . balance of the fifteenth anniversary. All of the details were covered, from having charities lined up as recipients of the anniversary proceeds to conducting a dinner in honor of Chef Girardet. This incredible tribute dinner was prepared by some of Chef Trotter's best friends, including Norman Van Aken, David Bouley, Gray Kunz, Guenter Seeger, Pierre Hermé, and Tetsuya Wakuda. The overriding theme from that weekend was one of sharing—sharing of culinary ideas, sharing of donations to charity, and sharing of love and friendship.

And there you have it. The background idea for *Workin' More Kitchen Sessions* and the companion show was set. The idea was that Chef Trotter would share his philosophy for cuisine in a way he has never done before.

Workin' more . . . energy: The show's twenty-six episodes were filmed in ten days at the studio kitchen of Charlie Trotter's restaurant. When I tell people this story, they often think I am bluffing. Honestly, one had to see it to believe it. The buzz in the room was so intense it was intoxicating. To see Chef Trotter literally create impromptu dishes was brilliant. Want to know his trick? Well, he's blessed to have an amazing recipe developer, Sari Zernich, as his partner. He and Sari are truly a yin and yang, the bass and the treble, the conductor and the orchestra.

I've often spent late nights talking with Charles about music. An avid jazz fan, Charles once said to me that he likes to think of himself as the Miles Davis of cuisine. The legendary trumpet

player once said that he never played a song the same way twice. That's the way that Charles approaches his cuisine. There are friends of the restaurant who have dined here hundreds of times and never had the same dish twice. My mind takes me to one amazing friend, Ray Harris. He has had over three hundred meals at Charlie Trotter's and never had the same dish twice. So I guess Charles is truly the Miles Davis of cuisine. . . workin' more ways to improvise with his cuisine, more ways to elevate the experience, more ways to please the guests.

Personally, I believe that Charles is so creative because he is so intellectual. His mind never stops yearning to learn. Whether the two of us are debating about mindfulness in Thich Nhat Hanh books or recalling compelling statements made by Henry Miller or Dostoyevsky, Charles and I have a blast. We have so much in common that I often call him "a mini-me." Watching Chef Trotter work and listening to him speak about cuisine and excellence have been some of the most intellectually stimulating experiences of my life.

Workin' more: love . . . Charles is one of the most generous individuals I know. He has a style that many don't really understand. At times he can seem very tough, but those of us who know him truly see the gentle inside the giant. He does not like to talk much of his philanthropy because he does it from the heart, not for the glory. He works hard, and he loves hard. If you are lucky enough to be a friend then you know what I mean. There is nothing that he deems impossible. His love for his son, for his parents, for his siblings, for his restaurant family, for his friends . . . it's something to behold.

So here is your chance to get intimate with Charles. See him workin' more . . . of his culinary magic . . . of his incredible passion for life . . . of his love for those close to him . . . of his dedication to charity . . . of his commitment to excellence. *Workin' More Kitchen Sessions with Charlie Trotter* is truly a gift, a chance to share the inspiration that went into creating this work of art.

One of Charles's favorite quotes is, "After love, there is only cuisine." I couldn't agree more! Thinking of Charles makes me think of amazing grace. Grace is unwarranted favor. In my world, that means "unwarranted favor from God." I have been graced to become a close friend of Charles . . . and I am thankful for the blessing.

Love,
Rochelle Smith
(Lifelong friend and colleague)

The parallels between cooking and playing music have always been extraordinarily intriguing to me. Both disciplines are grounded in the idea that once you understand classic, time-honored ways of how things work—ingredient combinations and cooking techniques here, note structures and lyricism there—you arrive at a place where it is more about just "being in the moment." The cook or musician who grasps the fundamentals is free to let go of conventions and cook or play in the same flowing way that a conversation unfolds.

Workin' More Kitchen Sessions with Charlie Trotter is an homage to such masters of musical spontaneity as Miles Davis, Charlie Parker, John Coltrane, Charles

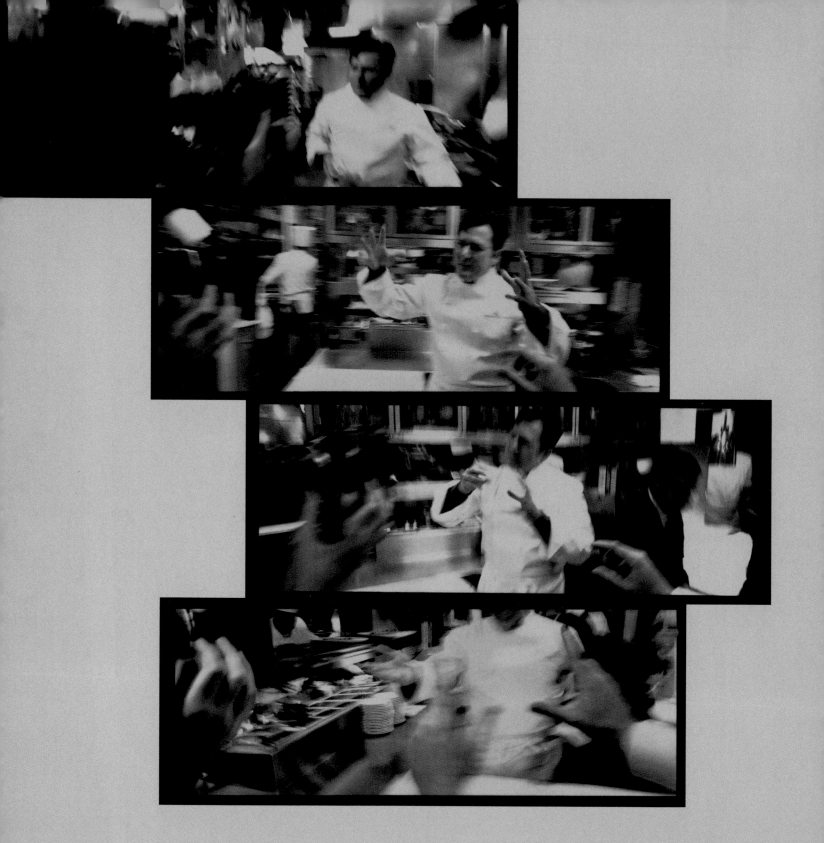

Mingus, Thelonious Monk, Sun Ra, and Bob Dylan. These artists epitomize what creativity is all about. Rather than relying on static "set pieces," they approached each bit of music like it was going to be experienced. Cooking can and should be looked at in the same way. After all, even the same ingredients vary from day to day, as does the mood you're in when you set about cooking. If you make a dish one way today, there's no reason you can't take a different approach to it tomorrow.

This book profiles the preparations that are featured on our *Kitchen Sessions* PBS series, but it's very much a work that exists independently of the program. The idea of both the book and the series is to give a glimpse into the inner workings of an intense, high-powered kitchen, but then to deconstruct and distill the basic culinary ideas. The hallmark of the cooking at Charlie Trotter's has always been the emphasis on the inter-changeability of foodstuffs. The recipes in this book are meant merely as guides, to be interpreted by the cook as the inspiration strikes. Perhaps salmon is featured in a given recipe, but you shouldn't hesitate to use chicken instead; morel mushrooms might be called for, but you can use button mushrooms if you feel like it, or even eliminate mushrooms altogether.

The only rule is to start with pristine seasonal products; after that, it's easy. Miles Davis said it best: "I'll play it first and tell you what it is later." Cooking is the same—let your palate be your guide!

ARTICHOKES

Artichokes Stuffed Three Ways

Serves 4

*The three fillings in this recipe are inspired pairings with artichokes.
The trio works together quite nicely on a single plate, or each filling could easily stand alone for
a less-involved effort. With the addition of a green salad, the dish is almost a meal in itself.
The components can be prepared in advance, then merely heated up
and assembled at the last moment. Feel free to devise your own presentation.*

EGGPLANT FILLING

1 small globe eggplant, halved lengthwise
Coarse salt
3 tablespoons extra virgin olive oil
1½ cups water
Salt and freshly ground black pepper
2 Japanese eggplants
8 cloves Roasted Garlic *(see Appendices)*,
  quartered

CUMIN RICE FILLING

2 tablespoons minced yellow onion
1 tablespoon butter
1 cup jasmine rice
1½ teaspoons cumin seeds,
  coarsely ground
2 cups Chicken Stock *(see Appendices)*
2 tablespoons brunoise-cut red bell pepper
2 tablespoons brunoise-cut yellow bell pepper
2 tablespoons chopped fresh chives
Salt and freshly ground black pepper
1 tablespoon freshly squeezed lemon juice
⅔ cup water

CURRIED DUCK FILLING

1 shallot, chopped
1 clove garlic, chopped
1 tablespoon chopped fresh ginger
1 stalk fresh lemongrass, finely chopped
2 tablespoons extra virgin olive oil
1 tablespoon hot curry powder
2 tablespoons sweet curry powder
1 teaspoon ground cumin
¼ cup tomato paste
1½ cups water
¼ cup chopped fresh cilantro
1 tablespoon freshly squeezed lime juice
Salt and freshly ground black pepper
2 teaspoons grapeseed oil
1 fresh duck breast, skin removed,
  cut into small dice
2 tablespoons small-diced mango

Continued

METHOD

To prepare the eggplant: Score the cut side of the globe eggplant; season heavily with coarse salt and let sit for 1 hour. Preheat the oven to 350°F. Rinse the salt from the eggplant and rub the cut side of the eggplant with 1 tablespoon of the olive oil. Place the eggplant, cut side down, in an ovenproof pan and add 1 cup of the water. Roast the eggplant for 45 minutes. Scrape the flesh from the skins and transfer to a blender with any juices that may remain in the pan. Add 1 tablespoon of the olive oil and the remaining ½ cup water; purée until smooth. Season to taste with salt and pepper. Cut the Japanese eggplants into small dice and place in a sauté pan with the remaining 1 tablespoon olive oil. Cook over medium heat for 3 to 4 minutes, or until just cooked through. Fold in the garlic; season to taste with salt and pepper.

To prepare the rice: Sauté the onion in the butter in a saucepan over medium heat until translucent, about 3 minutes. Add the rice and stir just to coat the rice. Add the cumin and stock; bring to a simmer. Decrease the heat to low and cover. Cook for 15 minutes, or until the rice is just cooked. Reserve 1 cup of the rice. Add the bell peppers and chives to the remaining rice; season to taste with salt and pepper. Place the reserved 1 cup of rice in a high-speed blender with the lemon juice and water. Purée until smooth and pass through a sieve; season the sauce to taste with salt and pepper.

To prepare the duck: Sauté the shallot, garlic, ginger, and lemongrass in the olive oil over medium heat for 5 minutes, or until the shallot is translucent. Add both curry powders, the cumin, and the tomato paste; cook for 2 minutes. Add the water and cilantro and cook for 10 minutes longer. Transfer to a blender and purée until smooth. Pass the sauce through a fine-mesh sieve. Add the lime juice and season to taste with salt and pepper. Heat the grapeseed oil in a sauté pan over medium heat. Season the duck meat with salt and pepper and cook in the pan for 2 minutes. Add half of the sauce and continue to cook until the duck is just cooked through, about 4 minutes. Fold in the mango. Warm the remaining sauce in a small saucepan and reserve for the assembly.

ARTICHOKES

Artichokes Stuffed Three Ways

6 small Braised Artichokes
  (see Appendices), halved
2 tablespoons butter
Salt and freshly ground black pepper

GARNISH

4 teaspoons Herb Oil *(see Appendices)*
4 sprigs young thyme, coarsely chopped
4 teaspoons micro cilantro, coarsely
  chopped (or chopped fresh cilantro)
Freshly ground black pepper

To prepare the artichokes: Place the artichokes cut side down in a sauté pan with the butter. Cook over medium heat until the artichokes are caramelized, about 3 minutes. Season to taste with salt and pepper.

ASSEMBLY

Spoon some of each of the 3 sauces at 3 separate points on each plate. Lay an artichoke half over each of the sauces in a random manner, with the stems pointing in different directions. On each plate, fill each artichoke with one of the fillings, matching the filling to the sauce and allowing it to cascade down into the sauce. Drizzle the Herb Oil around the plates and sprinkle with the thyme and cilantro. Top with pepper.

WINE NOTES

There are multiple layers of flavor in this dish, which can cause problems in selecting a perfect wine match. Choose a wine with a restrained style that acts as a background to tie all of the flavors together, rather than one that will contribute additional tastes. A tremendous pairing, and also interesting on its own, is a Junmai Ginjo sake called Southern Beauty. The delicate, low-acid flavors of this sake bind the eggplant and the curried duck together. And what better pairing for rice!

Artichoke and Tomato Turnover with Herb Purée

Serves 4

This preparation celebrates the heavenly trio of artichokes, tomatoes, and onions — though its crowning glory is the heady, explosively flavored herb purée, which gains a sensual mouthfeel from the addition of pecorino Romano cheese. It's a great make-ahead dish that can easily be popped into the oven just before the meal. The elegant approach below calls for crafting individual turnovers, but a single large turnover can also be made. One could add chunks of lobster meat or pieces of duck confit if a more substantial entrée is desired.

TOMATO FILLING

1 yellow onion, diced
3 tablespoons extra virgin olive oil
6 cloves Roasted Garlic *(see Appendices)*
4 tomatoes, cored and diced
2 sprigs thyme
3 bay leaves, crushed
1 tablespoon coriander seeds, crushed
1 teaspoon black peppercorns, crushed
Salt and freshly ground black pepper

ARTICHOKE FILLING

1 small red onion, julienned
2 raw artichoke bottoms, sliced into
⅛-inch wedges
2 tablespoons extra virgin olive oil
1 tablespoon balsamic vinegar
1½ cups loosely packed arugula
  leaves, washed
½ cup pine nuts, toasted
Salt and freshly ground black pepper

HERB PURÉE

1 cup loosely packed fresh basil
¼ cup loosely packed fresh flat-leaf parsley
¼ cup loosely packed fresh spinach leaves
1 clove garlic
½ cup extra virgin olive oil
½ cup grated pecorino Romano cheese
Salt and freshly ground black pepper

1½ pounds Cream Cheese Dough
  (see Appendices)
1 large egg, beaten
Salt and freshly ground black pepper

GARNISH

4 teaspoons balsamic vinegar

METHOD

To prepare the tomato filling: Sauté the onion in the olive oil over medium heat until translucent, about 5 minutes. Add the garlic, tomatoes, thyme, bay leaves, coriander, and peppercorns to the pan; cook over medium-low heat for 20 minutes, or until most of the liquid has evaporated. Remove from the heat and season to taste with salt and pepper. Let cool before using.

To prepare the artichoke filling: Place the onion, artichokes, and olive oil in a sauté pan and cook over medium heat for 15 minutes, or until the onion is caramelized and the artichokes are tender. Add the vinegar, arugula, and pine nuts; cook for 2 minutes. Remove from the heat and season to taste with salt and pepper. Let cool before using.

To prepare the herb purée: In a blender or food processor, purée the basil, parsley, spinach, garlic, and olive oil until smooth. Add the cheese; pulse to incorporate. Season to taste with salt and pepper.

To prepare the turnovers: Preheat the oven to 375°F. Roll out the dough to a ⅛-inch thickness, and cut into four 8-inch-diameter circles. Line a sheet pan with parchment paper. Lay the dough circles on the parchment-lined pan and brush lightly with some of the egg. Spoon 1½ tablespoons of the tomato mixture in the center of each dough circle. Spoon one-fourth of the artichoke filling over the tomato on each dough circle and fold the dough carefully in half. Press the edges with a fork to seal. Brush the outside of the turnovers with the egg and season with salt and pepper. Bake for 25 minutes, or until golden brown. Remove from oven and let sit for 3 minutes before slicing in half.

ASSEMBLY

Place 2 turnover halves on each plate and spoon the herb purée around them. Drizzle the balsamic vinegar around the herb purée.

WINE NOTES

At first thought, Sauvignon Blanc seemed to be right for this dish because of the herb purée. But when faced with the richness of the cream cheese crust, Sauvignon Blancs taste thin and poor. The wine needs to have a fatter texture while still maintaining at least a moderate level of acidity. Grüner Veltliner from the Wachau region of Austria boasts these attributes and also harmonizes with the artichokes and the arugula. Producers such as Prager and Knoll craft fine examples of this varietal.

Lamb Loin with Olive Oil–Poached Artichokes and Red Wine–Kalamata Olive Sauce

Serves 4

Of all the harmonious pairings of foodstuffs, artichokes and lamb certainly rank in the upper echelon. Here, with lentils for body and olives, capers, and red onion for zest, we have the makings of a heavenly dish. And while the sheer earthiness of this preparation may satisfy on a very basic level, the flavors are actually quite delicate. Coarse sea salt and a few leaves of chervil are all that are needed to round things out.

ARTICHOKES

2 raw artichoke bottoms with
  stems attached
2 cups extra virgin olive oil
3 sprigs thyme
2 cloves garlic, smashed
2 bay leaves
1 lemon, juiced
Salt and freshly ground black pepper

LAMB AND SAUCE

2 pounds lamb loin with extra fat
  slab attached
2 tablespoons puréed Kalamata olives
Salt and freshly ground black pepper
2 tablespoons grapeseed oil
1 cup red wine
1 cup julienned red onion
½ cup julienned red bell pepper
½ cup sliced Kalamata olives
½ cup Meat Stock Reduction
  (see Appendices)
2 tablespoons capers, rinsed and chopped
½ tablespoon balsamic vinegar
1½ tablespoons chopped fresh chives

GARNISH

1 cup freshly cooked French
  green lentils, hot
Freshly ground black pepper
4 teaspoons micro parsley or chervil leaves
  (or chopped fresh parsley or chervil)
4 teaspoons extra virgin olive oil

METHOD

To prepare the artichokes: Slice the artichokes into ⅓-inch-thick wedges. Place the artichokes in a small saucepan with the olive oil, thyme, garlic, bay leaves, and lemon juice; cook over low heat for 15 minutes, or until the artichokes are cooked al dente. Remove the artichokes from the pan to prevent overcooking. The artichokes can be prepared several hours ahead of time. Reheat them in the oil just prior to serving. Drain the artichokes and season to taste with salt and pepper at the last minute.

To prepare the lamb and sauce: Preheat the oven to 400°F. Rub the lamb loin with the olive purée and roll up in the attached fat slab, covering the whole loin. Secure with butcher's twine. Season the outside of the loin with salt and pepper. Heat the grapeseed oil in a roasting pan over high heat. Add the loin and sear on all sides until golden brown and crispy. Roast in the oven for 30 minutes, or until cooked to medium-rare. Transfer the lamb to a cutting board and let rest. Drain off any excess fat from the pan. Deglaze the pan on the stove top with the wine, then add the onion and cook for 3 to 4 minutes, or until the onion is tender. Add the bell pepper, sliced olives, stock reduction, capers, vinegar, and chives; cook for 3 minutes longer to bring the flavors together. Season to taste with salt and pepper. Remove the cooking twine from the lamb and cut into 1½-inch-thick medallions. Season to taste with salt and pepper.

ASSEMBLY

Spoon some of the lentils and artichokes in the center of each plate. Place a slice of the lamb atop the lentils and spoon the sauce around the plate. Top with pepper and sprinkle with the micro parsley. Drizzle the olive oil around the plate.

WINE NOTES

The brightness of the Red Wine–Kalamata Olive Sauce and the earthiness of the lamb direct the match to a Rioja from San Vicente. The brown spice notes of cumin and coriander from the San Vicente enhance the roasted flavors of the lamb. Another characteristic of wines from the Rioja region of Spain is their elevated level of acidity, which ties in precisely with the olive sauce.

Shaved Raw Artichokes with Pecorino Cheese and Pine Nuts

Serves 4

This is a fun and versatile salad that is very easy to prepare.
The flavors are light and clean, but at the same time they gently assert themselves.
Sometimes, to create a more substantial dish, I add a piece of sautéed fish or grilled chicken breast,
layering it on top of the ingredients.

ARTICHOKES

3 raw artichoke bottoms
2 cups water
3 tablespoons freshly squeezed lemon juice
3 tablespoons extra virgin olive oil
Salt and freshly ground black pepper

GARNISH

¼ cup finely grated pecorino
   Romano cheese
2 tablespoons chiffonade-cut fresh
   flat-leaf parsley
1 tablespoon minced shallot
2 red radishes, finely julienned
¼ cup pine nuts, toasted
¼ teaspoon finely grated lime zest
Freshly ground black pepper
4 teaspoons extra virgin olive oil

METHOD

To prepare the artichokes: Place the artichoke bottoms in the water with 2 tablespoons of the lemon juice and allow to sit for 2 hours. Remove from the water and cut each artichoke bottom in half. Using a mandoline, thinly slice the artichokes; toss with the olive oil and remaining 1 tablespoon lemon juice. Season with salt and pepper. Let stand in the marinade for 30 minutes.

ASSEMBLY

Cover the bottom of each plate with a thin layer of the artichokes. Sprinkle a fine layer of the cheese and parsley over the artichokes. Toss the shallot and radishes together and sprinkle over the plates. Sprinkle the pine nuts and lime zest over the plate. Top with pepper and drizzle with the olive oil.

WINE NOTES

The vivid acidity from the lemon juice and the earthy saltiness of pecorino Romano cheese are the keys to this dish. Round, low-acid, off-dry wines such as Pinot Gris taste flabby when faced with the brightness of the lemon juice. An ideal wine needs to be dry, crisp, and fruity—the calling cards of Austrian Riesling. Knoll's Smaragd Trocken "Ried Loibenberg" has a medium- to full-bodied style that isn't dominated by the strong flavors of the cheese. Knoll's Riesling lightens the lemon juice tones and adds a layer of minerality to the artichokes.

Hamachi with Artichoke Soup, Rapini, and Saffron Aioli

Serves 4

Although this soup is satiny and quite subtle in its flavor, it nevertheless has a sensual, hearty appeal as well. The addition of the hamachi makes the dish more of an appetizer than a soup; tuna or chicken could also be used. The saffron aioli provides a haunting note of exotic spice, while just-softened rapini lends a profound depth in both texture and flavor. This would be an ideal beginning for a special dinner.

SAFFRON AIOLI
1 teaspoon slightly crushed saffron threads
2 tablespoons white wine
1 tablespoon freshly squeezed lemon juice
1 large egg yolk
1 cup grapeseed oil
Salt and freshly ground black pepper

SOUP
8 Braised Artichokes *(see Appendices)*
3 cups Vegetable Stock *(see Appendices)*
3 tablespoons extra virgin olive oil
2 teaspoons rice wine vinegar
1 teaspoon minced garlic
Salt and freshly ground black pepper
1 tablespoon butter

HAMACHI
2 teaspoons grapeseed oil
4 3-ounce hamachi fillets
Salt and freshly ground black pepper

RAPINI
2 cups rapini florets, blanched
1 tablespoon butter
1 teaspoon minced garlic
Salt and freshly ground black pepper

GARNISH
¼ cup micro herbs (or chopped fresh herbs such as thyme and parsley)
4 teaspoons Saffron Oil *(see Appendices)*
Freshly ground black pepper

METHOD
To prepare the aioli: Heat the saffron in the wine for 30 seconds or until the flavors have bloomed. Add the lemon juice and transfer to a mixing bowl. Add the egg yolk and whisk together. Slowly drizzle in the grapeseed oil, whisking vigorously until fully incorporated (this can also be done using a handheld blender). Season to taste with salt and pepper.

To prepare the soup: Chop 6 of the artichokes and purée them in a blender with the stock, olive oil, vinegar, and garlic until smooth. Transfer to a saucepan and warm over medium heat. Season the soup to taste with salt and pepper. Slice the remaining 2 artichokes into eighths. Heat a nonstick pan over high heat; add the butter and the artichoke pieces. Cook until the artichokes are golden brown, about 4 minutes; season to taste with salt and pepper, and reserve for the assembly.

To prepare the hamachi: Heat the grapeseed oil in a sauté pan over high heat. Season the hamachi with salt and pepper and add to the pan. Cook for 3 minutes, then flip the hamachi over and cook for 1 to 2 minutes, or until just underdone.

To prepare the rapini: Just prior to use, sauté the rapini in the butter with the garlic over medium heat for 2 to 3 minutes, or until hot. Season to taste with salt and pepper.

ASSEMBLY
Arrange some of the rapini and caramelized artichoke pieces in the center of each wide, shallow bowl. Ladle in some of the soup and rest a piece of the hamachi atop the vegetables. Spoon some of the aioli over the hamachi and drizzle it around the bowl. Sprinkle the micro herbs around the bowl and drizzle the Saffron Oil around the soup. Top with pepper.

WINE NOTES
The artichoke soup is rich in texture and flavor, and even more weight is added by the hamachi and the saffron aioli. The partner for this soup needs to be a round wine that is full-bodied and has an almost chewy texture. Whites made from Marsanne and Roussanne grapes fit these requirements perfectly, especially when they come from the Hermitage appellation of the Rhône Valley. Oaky California versions of these wines would not work as effectively, because the soup can cause them to taste bitter.

Halibut and Artichokes
en Papillote

Serves 4

*One of my favorite ways to cook is to wrap everything together in a tidy little packet.
The ingredients and aromatics marry perfectly in this most gentle of cooking methods.
Here the artichokes are the star of the show, providing a depth of flavor that supports all the remaining elements.
For a heartier dish, substitute small strips of steak for the halibut.*

FILLING

12 baby artichokes, cleaned and
   cut into sixths
2 tablespoons extra virgin olive oil
1 tablespoon freshly squeezed lemon juice
Salt and freshly ground black pepper
1 cup thinly sliced leeks (white part only)
4 baby turnips, peeled and halved
8 pattypan squash, halved
4 baby carrots, peeled and quartered
4 2½-ounce halibut fillet pieces
4 teaspoons butter
1 tablespoon chopped fresh tarragon
2 tablespoons grated lemon zest

SHALLOT-HERB VINAIGRETTE

1 shallot, minced
1 tablespoon chopped fresh tarragon
1 tablespoon chopped fresh flat-leaf parsley
1 tablespoon chopped fresh chives
2 tablespoons freshly squeezed
   lemon juice
¼ cup extra virgin olive oil
Salt and freshly ground black pepper

METHOD

To prepare the filling: Preheat the oven to 425°F. Toss the artichokes with the olive oil and lemon juice; season to taste with salt and pepper. Cut 4 sheets of nonabsorbent parchment paper into 12-inch hearts. Fold the parchment hearts in half, creating a seam; lightly oil the inside of each heart. Place one-fourth of the artichokes, leeks, turnips, squash, and carrots on one side of each heart and set the halibut on top.

Place 1 teaspoon of the butter over each piece of halibut and sprinkle with the tarragon and lemon zest. Make sure the filling is at least 1½ inches from the edge of the heart. Fold the empty half of the heart over the fish and fold and crimp the edges of the paper to form a tight seal. Place the parchment packets on a heavy-bottomed sheet pan or sizzle platter and bake until the packets are highly puffed and the paper is browned, 12 to 15 minutes.

To prepare the vinaigrette: Place the shallot, herbs, and lemon juice in a small saucepan; slowly whisk in the olive oil. Warm over medium-low heat until just warm and season to taste with salt and pepper.

ASSEMBLY

Immediately after removing the packets from the oven, transfer 1 to each plate. Cut open and roll back the parchment with a fork. Spoon some of the vinaigrette over the halibut.

WINE NOTES

The delicate flavors of the halibut and artichokes call for a light- to medium-bodied wine. A California Sauvignon Blanc, like Crocker & Starr from the Napa Valley, has both the acidity to balance with the lively shallot-herb vinaigrette and some green, grassy notes that are reflected in the squash and tarragon. At the same time, this Sauvignon Blanc inserts a layer of tropical fruit that provides an interesting contrast.

Shrimp and Corn Cake
Serves 4

*This hearty shrimp and corn cake can work either as a course on its own or as a succulent side dish.
The flavors from the bacon, shrimp, and corn meld perfectly. Additional elements such as
zucchini, bell pepper, and celery provide interesting flavor and texture notes.
It also makes a superb breakfast dish the next morning — that is, if there is anything left over!*

CORN BREAD

2 cups egg whites (from about 16
   large eggs)
1 cup flour
⅔ cup cornmeal
2 tablespoons sugar
2 teaspoons salt
1 cup milk
2 teaspoons extra virgin olive oil

SHRIMP AND CORN CAKE

1 cup crème fraîche
3 large eggs
Salt and freshly ground black pepper
1 cup small-diced bacon
6 ears of sweet corn, kernels removed
   and reserved
½ cup chopped scallions
1 tablespoon chopped Roasted Garlic
   (see Appendices)
¼ cup small-diced celery
¼ cup small-diced zucchini
½ cup small-diced red bell pepper
¼ cup small-diced yellow
   crookneck squash
30 small shrimp, peeled, deveined,
   and halved
1 tablespoon crushed red pepper
1½ cups Chicken Stock *(see Appendices)*
Corn bread (above)

SAUCE

¼ cup minced shallot
2 tablespoons butter
1 jalapeño chile, seeded and minced
1 cup Chicken Stock *(see Appendices)*
½ cup crème fraîche
2 tablespoons chopped fresh chives
Salt and freshly ground black pepper

METHOD

To prepare the corn bread: Preheat the oven to 350°F. In the bowl of an electric mixer fitted
with the whisk attachment, whip the egg whites on medium speed to form stiff peaks, 3 to 4
minutes. Mix the flour, cornmeal, sugar, and salt together in a large bowl. Add the milk and
olive oil. Fold in the whipped egg whites. Line a 9 by 5-inch loaf pan with parchment paper
and lightly butter the paper. Pour the batter into the prepared loaf pan and bake for 25 minutes,
or until a tester inserted in the center comes out clean. Cool to room temperature and cut
into large dice.

To prepare the shrimp and corn cake: Whisk together the crème fraîche and eggs; season
with salt and pepper. Preheat the oven to 300°F. Render the fat from the bacon in a large
cast-iron pan over medium-low heat, 7 to 10 minutes. Add the vegetables, shrimp, and
crushed red pepper; cook for 10 minutes over medium-high heat, or until the vegetables are
tender but not caramelized. Add the stock and simmer for 5 minutes. Fold in the corn bread
and the crème fraîche mixture; bake the batter in the skillet for 45 to 60 minutes, or until
golden brown.

To prepare the sauce: Place the shallot and butter in a sauté pan and cook over medium
heat until translucent, about 3 minutes. Add the chile and continue to cook for 2 minutes.
Add the stock and bring to a simmer. Remove from the heat and slowly whisk in the crème
fraîche and chives. Season to taste with salt and pepper.

ASSEMBLY

Either serve the corn cake family style right out of the pan, or place a portion in the center
of each plate and spoon the sauce on and around it.

WINE NOTES

As a general rule, it is difficult to pair full-bodied, oaky California Chardonnays with food,
but this hefty presentation proves to be the exception. The Gallo "Estate" Chardonnay
is a remarkable match with the smoky bacon notes and rich corn cake. The wine's balance
also allows the shrimp to add mineral tones to the full-flavored course.

Grilled Tuna with Sweet Corn Relish, Avocado Purée, and Cilantro Vinaigrette

Serves 4

Light and clean but absolutely packed with flavor, this preparation is a marriage of contrasts. The sweet corn relish explodes with a delicate spiciness and intoxicating sweet and sour flavors. A luscious avocado purée helps to tame the relish while providing a creamy richness. One, two, or three pieces of grilled tuna can be placed on the purée depending on whether you desire a smaller course — an appetizer, say — or a full-blown entrée. Pork tenderloin or Cornish game hen would make wonderful substitutes for the tuna.

CORN RELISH

¼ cup small-diced yellow onion
1 tablespoon minced garlic
1 tablespoon minced jalapeño chile
1 tablespoon grapeseed oil
1½ cups sweet corn kernels
¼ cup small-diced red bell pepper
¼ cup small-diced yellow bell pepper
2 tablespoons small-diced yellow
    crookneck squash
2 tablespoons small-diced zucchini
2 red Thai chiles, minced
1 tablespoon maple sugar
1 tablespoon lime juice
2 tablespoons white wine vinegar
Salt and freshly ground black pepper

AVOCADO PURÉE

1 ripe avocado, peeled, pitted, and chopped
1 lime, juiced
1 jalapeño chile, seeded and chopped
2 tablespoons finely chiffonade-cut
    fresh cilantro
½ to ¾ cup water
Salt and freshly ground black pepper

CILANTRO VINAIGRETTE

2 tablespoons minced shallot
3 tablespoons freshly squeezed lime juice
1 tablespoon tequila
10 tablespoons extra virgin olive oil
¼ cup finely chiffonade-cut fresh cilantro
Salt and freshly ground black pepper

TUNA

4 tuna fillet pieces (3 inches long and
    1 inch square)
1 tablespoon grapeseed oil
Salt and freshly ground black pepper

METHOD

To prepare the corn relish: Sauté the onion, garlic, and jalapeño chile in the oil over medium heat for 2 minutes. Add the corn and other vegetables, the maple sugar, lime juice, and vinegar; cook for 5 minutes, or until the corn is tender. Season to taste with salt and pepper.

To prepare the avocado purée: Purée the avocado, lime juice, chile, and cilantro in a blender with ½ cup of the water until the mixture is smooth and has a thick, saucelike consistency. Add additional water if necessary. Season to taste with salt and pepper.

To prepare the vinaigrette: Place the shallot, lime juice, and tequila in a bowl; slowly whisk in the olive oil. Fold in the cilantro and season to taste with salt and pepper.

To prepare the tuna: Prepare a hot grill. Rub the tuna on all sides with the oil and season with salt and pepper. Grill the tuna for 2 minutes on each side, until just seared on the outside but still rare. Cut the tuna pieces in half crosswise and season again.

ASSEMBLY

Spoon a straight line of the avocado purée across the center of each plate. Place 2 pieces of the tuna, cut side up, in the center of the plate. Spoon the corn relish around the tuna. Drizzle the vinaigrette over the tuna and around the plate. Top with freshly ground black pepper.

WINE NOTES

This entrée has many different angles that require attention in order to achieve a magical wine pairing. There are green, herby notes in the cilantro vinaigrette, while the purée of avocado and the oily tuna add weight and richness. A suitable wine needs to have a high level of acidity to handle the vinaigrette as well as to slice through the depth of the avocado and tuna. A crisp, medium-bodied wine like Silex, a Pouilly-Fumé from Didier Dagueneau that has seen a touch of oak aging, simultaneously complements the cilantro and adds a layer of minerality to the tuna.

Halibut with Yellow Corn Grits and Red Wine–Corn Sauce

Serves 4

Though in some ways quite earthy, with the yellow corn grits and the black trumpet mushrooms, this dish is at the same time very refined. A drizzle of red wine–corn sauce provides a clean, decisive acidic note that weaves all these full-bodied components together. Adjust the portion size as you see fit to make an appetizer or an entrée. If the grits are smoothed out on a baking sheet, then cooled for several hours or overnight, disks or other cut-out shapes can be sautéed into crispy galettes. Don't hesitate to use beef tenderloin in lieu of the halibut.

RED WINE–CORN SAUCE

1 cup sweet corn kernels
2 tablespoons minced shallot
1 tablespoon extra virgin olive oil
½ cup Red Wine Reduction
  (see Appendices)
½ teaspoon white wine vinegar
Salt and freshly ground black pepper

GRITS

3 tablespoons minced shallot
1 clove garlic, minced
1 tablespoon extra virgin olive oil
2 cups sweet corn kernels
1 tablespoon butter
2 cups cooked yellow corn grits, warm
Salt and freshly ground black pepper

MUSHROOMS

2 tablespoons butter
1 tablespoon minced shallot
2 cups black trumpet mushrooms, cleaned
1 teaspoon balsamic vinegar
¼ cup Chicken Stock *(see Appendices)*
Salt and freshly ground black pepper

HALIBUT

1 tablespoon grapeseed oil
4 3-ounce halibut pieces
Salt and freshly ground black pepper

GARNISH

4 teaspoons extra virgin olive oil
4 teaspoons chopped fresh chervil
Freshly ground black pepper

METHOD

To prepare the sauce: Sauté the corn and shallot in the olive oil over medium heat for 5 minutes, or until the corn is tender. Add the wine reduction and vinegar; cook for 5 minutes longer. Purée in a blender until smooth, then pass through a fine-mesh sieve. Season to taste with salt and pepper.

To prepare the grits: Sauté the shallot and garlic in the olive oil over medium heat until translucent, about 3 minutes. Add the corn and butter; continue to cook for 5 minutes, or until the corn is tender. Fold in the cooked grits and season to taste with salt and pepper.

To prepare the mushrooms: Place the butter and shallot in a sauté pan and cook over medium heat until the shallots are translucent, about 2 minutes. Add the mushrooms and cook for 3 minutes. Add the vinegar and stock; cook for 3 to 5 minutes, or until the mushrooms are just tender. Season to taste with salt and pepper. Divide the mushrooms in half and reserve any pan juices. Finely chop half of the mushrooms.

To prepare the halibut: Heat the grapeseed oil in a sauté pan over high heat. Season the halibut with salt and pepper and add to the pan. Cook for 3 minutes on each side, or until just cooked through.

ASSEMBLY

Place a spoonful of the grits in the center of each plate. Place a piece of the halibut on top and cover with the finely chopped mushrooms. Spoon the sauce around the grits. Place the remaining black trumpet mushrooms at 6 points around the sauce. Drizzle the reserved juices from the sauté pan around the grits. Spoon the olive oil around the plate and sprinkle with the chopped chervil. Top with pepper.

WINE NOTES

With the addition of black trumpet mushrooms and a red wine-based sauce, the halibut is given more body and becomes a red wine-friendly dish. Littorai Pinot Noir from the Hirsch Vineyard is a medium-bodied wine that accents the wine in the corn sauce without dominating the flavor of the halibut. Its red berry and cherry notes provide a fantastic contrast to the earthy black trumpets.

Smoked Chicken Salad with Corn Vinaigrette

Serves 4

This light salad is ideal for a summertime luncheon. Smoked chicken and sweet corn seem meant for each other. Wild rice and bell peppers add additional flavors and textures. Try substituting grilled shrimp or lobster for equally stunning results.

SMOKED CHICKEN

3 skinless, boneless chicken breasts
2 cups Pickling Brine *(see Appendices)*
1 tablespoon grapeseed oil
Freshly ground black pepper
2 cups dry hickory chips plus 1 cup hickory chips soaked overnight in water to cover, then drained

CORN VINAIGRETTE

¼ cup small-diced red onion
¾ cup extra virgin olive oil
1 cup sweet corn kernels
3 tablespoons sherry wine vinegar
2 tablespoons chopped fresh chives
Salt and freshly ground black pepper

SALAD

2 cups cooked wild rice
¼ cup small-diced roasted red bell pepper
¼ cup small-diced roasted yellow bell pepper
3 scallions, finely sliced diagonally
½ cup sweet corn kernels, cooked
Salt and freshly ground black pepper

METHOD

To prepare the chicken: Soak the chicken breasts in the brine for 4 hours and drain. Prepare a medium-hot grill. Brush the chicken with the grapeseed oil and season with the pepper. Place the dry hickory chips over the hot coals in the grill. When the dry chips catch fire, sprinkle the wet chips over the coals. Place the chicken breasts on the grill and cover tightly with the grill lid. Smoke for 5 minutes; turn the chicken over and smoke for 5 to 7 minutes longer, or until cooked through. Remove the chicken from the grill and slice ¼ inch thick.

To prepare the vinaigrette: Sauté the onion in 1 tablespoon of the olive oil over medium heat for 5 minutes, or until translucent. Add the corn and continue to cook until the corn is tender, about 5 minutes. Add the remaining olive oil, the vinegar, and the chives. Season to taste with salt and pepper.

To prepare the salad: Combine the wild rice, bell peppers, scallions, and corn in a bowl. Fold in half of the corn vinaigrette and season to taste with salt and pepper.

ASSEMBLY

Place a 4-inch ring mold in the center of each plate. Spoon some of the salad into the ring molds and press down firmly. Remove the ring molds and arrange some of the sliced chicken atop the salad in a pinwheel shape. Spoon the remaining corn vinaigrette over the chicken and around the plate. Top with freshly ground black pepper.

WINE NOTES

Duckhorn's Sauvignon Blanc, though often in the shadow of this vintner's Merlot and Cabernet Sauvignon, is a wine that deserves attention. The touch of oak aging that the Duckhorn receives brings out the smokiness of the chicken, but the wine also has a crisp acidity that keeps the corn vinaigrette light and buoyant. Rudd makes a similar Sauvignon Blanc, albeit with a slightly fuller body, that also works well with the smoked chicken.

Grouper with Porcini Mushrooms, White Asparagus, Prosciutto, and Sweet Corn Emulsion

Serves 4

While there are certainly rich notes here—the grouper, the mushrooms, the prosciutto—the whole leaves an overwhelmingly airy impression, primarily because of the sweet corn emulsion. Mixing components that are earthy and ethereal in a single dish can yield memorable results. If grouper is unavailable, practically any fish can work in its place, as can chicken or pork.

MUSHROOMS AND SAUCE
1 shallot, peeled and minced
½ teaspoon minced garlic
3 tablespoons butter
3 cups porcini mushrooms, cut into eighths
1 sprig thyme
1 cup water
Salt and freshly ground black pepper

CORN EMULSION
½ cup chopped yellow onion
2 cups sweet corn kernels
6 tablespoons butter
2½ cups Corn Water *(see Appendices)*
1 tablespoon ground cumin
Salt and freshly ground black pepper

VEGETABLES
2 tablespoons minced shallot
1 tablespoon extra virgin olive oil
1 leek (white part only), cleaned and cut
   into ¼-inch-thick rings
12 pencil-thin stalks white asparagus, peeled
   and cut diagonally into 2-inch-long pieces
½ cup sweet corn kernels
½ cup Vegetable Stock *(see Appendices)*
1 bay leaf
1 sprig rosemary
4 ounces prosciutto, julienned
Salt and freshly ground black pepper
1 tablespoon chopped fresh basil

GROUPER
1 tablespoon grapeseed oil
4 4-ounce grouper fillets
Salt and freshly ground black pepper

GARNISH
4 teaspoons globe basil leaves

METHOD

To prepare the mushrooms and sauce: Heat the shallot, garlic, and butter in a sauté pan over medium heat for 2 minutes, or until the shallot is translucent. Add the mushrooms and cook for 3 minutes longer. Add the thyme and ¼ cup of the water; cook until the mushrooms are just tender. Reserve two-thirds of the mushrooms. Purée the remaining mushrooms in a blender with just enough water (about ¾ cup) to make a thick sauce. Season both the mushrooms and the sauce to taste with salt and pepper. Reheat the sauce just prior to use in a small saucepan.

To prepare the emulsion: In a saucepan over medium heat, sauté the onion and corn in 2 tablespoons of the butter for 4 to 5 minutes, or until just tender. Add the Corn Water and cumin. Bring to a simmer and cook for 5 minutes. Purée in a blender and strain through a fine-mesh sieve into a saucepan. Whisk in the remaining 4 tablespoons butter and season to taste with salt and pepper. Using a handheld blender, froth just prior to use until a thick foam develops.

To prepare the vegetables: Sauté the shallot in the olive oil over medium heat for 2 minutes, or until the shallot is translucent. Add the leek and continue to cook for 3 minutes. Add the asparagus, corn, stock, bay leaf, and rosemary. Bring to a simmer and cook for 5 minutes, or until the asparagus is cooked al dente. Add the prosciutto to the pan and cook for 2 minutes, or until all the flavors have melded. Season to taste with salt and pepper and stir in the basil.

To prepare the grouper: Heat the grapeseed oil in a sauté pan over high heat. Season the grouper with salt and pepper and add to the pan. Cook for 3 minutes on each side, or until just cooked through.

ASSEMBLY
Place some of the mushrooms and vegetables in the center of each plate. Spoon a large ring of the mushroom sauce around the vegetables. Place a piece of the grouper atop the vegetables. Spoon some of the corn emulsion foam over the grouper and sprinkle the globe basil around the plate.

WINE NOTES
Because this course has light flavors from the white asparagus and leeks, but also the more powerful flavors of porcini mushrooms and prosciutto, the appropriate wine needs to be nimble. Domaine Ramonet's Chassagne-Montrachet "Les Caillerets" is an impeccably balanced white Burgundy that has the ability to enhance the richness of the ham without leaving the vegetables behind. The stony notes of the wine are excellent with the sautéed grouper.

Grilled–Sweet Corn Soup with Crabmeat-Corn Napoleon and Shellfish Oil

Serves 4

The elements of this dish can be presented formally, as here; or else the crab, corn kernels, wilted arugula, and pearl onions can be stirred into the soup and served as a chowder. Either way, the flavors are clean and explosive. Add chiles if you desire something with more kick.

SOUP

6 ears of sweet corn in their husks, soaked 3 hours in water
1 small yellow onion, peeled and cut into ½-inch rings
2 tablespoons extra virgin olive oil
3 cups Corn Water *(see Appendices)*
Salt and freshly ground black pepper

CRAB

1 cup crabmeat
1 tablespoon freshly squeezed lime juice
2 tablespoons chopped fresh chives
Salt and freshly ground black pepper

PEARL ONIONS

10 purple pearl onions, peeled
10 white pearl onions, peeled
2 cups Chicken Stock *(see Appendices)*
1 tablespoon white wine vinegar
Salt and freshly ground black pepper

GARNISH

2 cups firmly packed arugula, blanched
8 lime segments, supremed and cut into thirds
4 teaspoons Shellfish Oil *(see Appendices)*
4 teaspoons chopped fresh cilantro
Freshly ground black pepper

METHOD

To prepare the soup: Prepare a medium-hot grill. Place the corn on the grill for 7 minutes on each side, or until the husks are charred and the corn is cooked. Lightly brush the onion rings with 1 tablespoon of the olive oil and grill for 5 minutes on each side, or until the onions are tender. Remove from the grill and chop coarsely. Remove the husks from the corn and cut off the kernels. Reserve 1 cup of the corn for the assembly. Purée the remaining corn in a blender with the Corn Water and the remaining 1 tablespoon olive oil until smooth. Season to taste with salt and pepper and strain through a fine-mesh sieve if fibrous. Reheat the soup just prior to serving.

To prepare the crab: Gently combine the crabmeat, lime juice, and chives; season to taste with salt and pepper.

To prepare the onions: Place all the onions, the stock, and the vinegar in a sauté pan over high heat. Cook the onions until the stock is reduced to a glaze and the onions have caramelized, about 25 minutes. Season to taste with salt and pepper.

ASSEMBLY

Place a 3-inch ring mold in the center of each shallow serving bowl. Place a small amount of the grilled onion in the bottom of the mold. Top with some of the arugula, crab mixture, grilled corn kernels, grilled onion, and more arugula; finally, top with a layer of the crab mixture. Ladle some of the hot soup around the mold and carefully remove the mold. Place 5 pearl onions and some of the lime segments in each bowl and drizzle the Shellfish Oil around the soup. Sprinkle with the cilantro and top with pepper.

WINE NOTES

Most people think only of red wine when Bordeaux is mentioned, but a wealth of world-class white is produced there as well. The combination of Sémillon and Sauvignon Blanc—the traditional blend in Bordeaux—is a versatile weapon in a wine and food–pairing arsenal. With the corn soup, Château Larrivet Haut-Brion from Pessac-Léognan is a stunning companion to the mineral note of the crab and the green flavor of the arugula. The Larrivet also has enough body to match the power of the soup, which overwhelms any lighter whites.

FENNEL

Mussel, Shrimp, and Fennel Chowder

Serves 4

This chowder is an extremely versatile preparation: lobster, scallops, and oysters can all be used in addition to or in place of the mussels and shrimp. Or for something completely different, place a piece of poached or steamed fish in a wide, flat bowl and spoon ¹/₃ cup of the chowder over the top. It can even be used as a sauce! The chowder can be prepared a day or two in advance.

FENNEL PURÉE

2 fennel bulbs, tops trimmed
2 sprigs thyme
2 bay leaves
1 cup milk
1 cup water
Salt and freshly ground black pepper

CHOWDER

1 cup small-diced bacon
½ cup small-diced yellow onion
2 cups small-diced peeled
   Yukon Gold potatoes
1 cup small-diced peeled carrot
1 cup small-diced celery
2 cups small-diced fennel
Fennel purée (above)
1 cup heavy whipping cream
50 mussels, scrubbed and debearded
20 medium shrimp, shelled, deveined,
   and cut into thirds
1½ cups mussel juice
1 lemon, juiced
Salt and freshly ground black pepper

GARNISH

2 tablespoons coarsely chopped
   fennel fronds
4 teaspoons Shellfish Oil *(see Appendices)*
Freshly ground black pepper

METHOD

To prepare the fennel purée: Preheat the oven to 350°F. Wrap the fennel bulbs, thyme, and bay leaves in aluminum foil. Place in an ovenproof pan and roast for 2 hours, or until the fennel is tender. Discard the bay leaves and thyme. Chop the fennel and purée in a blender with the milk and water. Pass through a fine-mesh sieve and season to taste with salt and pepper.

To prepare the chowder: Sauté the bacon in a large saucepan over medium heat until all the fat is rendered, 5 to 7 minutes. Add the onion and potatoes; cook over medium-high heat for 5 minutes. Lower the heat to medium and add the carrot, celery, and diced fennel. Cook for 5 minutes. Add the fennel purée and heavy cream; cook for 5 minutes longer. Add the mussels, shrimp, and mussel juice; simmer for 5 to 7 minutes, or until the mussels have opened and the shrimp is just cooked. Discard any unopened mussels. Remove the mussels from their shells if desired and return them to the chowder. Season the chowder with the lemon juice and salt and pepper just prior to serving.

ASSEMBLY

Ladle some of the chowder into each bowl and sprinkle with the fennel fronds. Drizzle the Shellfish Oil around the chowder and top with pepper.

WINE NOTES

A full-bodied white Burgundy, such as a Meursault or a Corton-Charlemagne, pushes this dish to a whole new level. The serving temperature of white Burgundies is particularly important. To be the most expressive, they are best served between 55°F and 60°F, which is far above the 33°F you will get if the wine has been buried in ice. When too cold, a Meursault from Château Genot-Boulanger "Les Bouchères" slices through the flavors of the chowder, masking all the smokiness from the bacon and fennel. At its proper temperature, the wine is glorious! More nuttiness and spice notes show themselves, and the wine has a rounder texture that ties these flavors together.

Braised Lamb Shank with Caramelized Fennel and Apricots

Serves 4

*Succulent braised lamb shanks are splendidly offset by luscious and delicately sweet
caramelized fennel and apricots. The flavors are homey and very satisfying. If you serve the shanks
with a simple salad and a side dish of risotto or buttered noodles, you won't need much more.
For a more exotic result, try adding a tablespoon or two of curry powder to the shanks at the outset of their braising.*

LAMB SHANKS

4 lamb shanks
Salt and freshly ground black pepper
1½ tablespoons extra virgin olive oil
1 yellow onion, coarsely chopped
1 carrot, peeled and coarsely chopped
1 stalk celery, coarsely chopped
1 head garlic, peeled and coarsely chopped
1 cup red wine
1 cup chopped dried apricots
2 quarts Chicken Stock *(see Appendices)*
2 fresh apricots, thinly sliced
1½ teaspoons sherry wine vinegar

FENNEL

2 large fennel bulbs, tops trimmed and
   bulbs cut into eighths
2 tablespoons extra virgin olive oil
2 bay leaves
2 sprigs thyme
2 dried red Thai chiles
1 tablespoon sugar
3 tablespoons sherry wine vinegar
4 fresh apricots, cut into eighths
2 tablespoons butter
Salt and freshly ground black pepper

GARNISH

¼ cup chopped fennel fronds

METHOD

To prepare the lamb shanks: Preheat the oven to 275˚F. Season the shanks with salt and pepper. Sear the shanks in the olive oil in a large roasting pan over medium-high heat for 10 minutes, or until browned on all sides. Remove the shanks and set aside. Add the onion, carrot, celery, and garlic to the same pan and cook for 10 minutes, or until golden brown. Deglaze the pan with the wine, add the dried apricots, and return the lamb shanks to the pan. Add the stock, cover tightly, and braise in the oven for 6 to 8 hours, or until the meat is very tender. Remove the lamb shanks from the pan. Strain the braising liquid through a fine-mesh sieve and cook over medium-low heat for 30 minutes, or until reduced to 2 cups. Add the fresh apricots and vinegar and cook for 5 minutes.

To prepare the fennel: Preheat the oven to 400˚F. Place the fennel, olive oil, bay leaves, thyme, and chiles in a roasting pan and roast uncovered for 15 minutes. Add the sugar, vinegar, fresh apricots, and butter. Cover, decrease the heat to 325˚F, and continue to roast for 15 minutes longer, or until the fennel is caramelized and tender. Season to taste with salt and pepper.

ASSEMBLY

Arrange 1 lamb shank and some of the fennel mixture in the center of each plate. Spoon the reduced braising liquid over the lamb shank and around the plate. Sprinkle with the fennel fronds.

WINE NOTES

Braised dishes are known for their heartiness and richness. The addition of apricots brings a sweet contrast to the meatiness of the lamb. In order to balance both the earthy lamb shank and the apricots, the wine should be fruit-forward but from the Old World. Modern producers like Domaine Les Paillères of Gigondas and Jamet of Côte-Rôtie make wines with enough stuffing to be delicious companions to this dish.

Italian Sausage and Fennel Focaccia

Serves 4

You could almost eat this focaccia like a sandwich, that's how lusty and full flavored it is.
For a light accompaniment, try serving it with a simple
garden salad or perhaps a piece of fish. Any leftovers are a great treat the next day.

FOCACCIA DOUGH

½ ounce active dry yeast
2½ cups warm water (about 120°F)
3 tablespoons extra virgin olive oil
6½ cups bread flour
½ teaspoon salt
¼ cup chopped fennel fronds

FILLING

3 fennel bulbs, tops trimmed and
   bulbs julienned
1 red onion, julienned
¼ cup extra virgin olive oil
2 pounds Italian sausage, broken into
   small pieces
¼ cup Roasted Garlic cloves
   (see Appendices)
2 tablespoons fennel seeds
2 tablespoons fresh thyme leaves

Extra virgin olive oil for brushing
Cornmeal for dusting

METHOD

To prepare the focaccia dough: Sprinkle the yeast into ½ cup of the warm water in the bowl of an electric mixer and let sit for 3 minutes. Whisk the remaining 2 cups water with the olive oil and set aside. Combine the flour and salt in a bowl and set aside. Pour the water-oil mixture over the yeast mixture and stir to blend. Add half the dry ingredients and stir with a rubber spatula to combine. Add the fennel fronds and the remaining dry ingredients and mix with the dough hook on low for 4 minutes, or until the dough comes together in a mass. (If the dough is dry, add a few more drops of water.) Continue to mix the dough for 16 minutes to develop the gluten. Remove the dough from the mixer and work it into a ball. Place the dough in an oiled bowl and brush the top of the dough with oil. Cover the bowl tightly with plastic wrap. Allow the dough to rise at room temperature until it doubles in size, about 1 hour. Punch down the dough to deflate it and then let it rise again until it doubles in size, about 1 hour. Punch down the dough again to deflate it. Divide the dough into 2 equal portions; place each in an oiled 1-gallon resealable plastic bag and refrigerate for 24 hours.

Remove the dough from the refrigerator. Place the dough on a lightly floured surface and dust with flour. Cover loosely with plastic wrap and let sit for 1½ hours.

To prepare the filling: Sauté the fennel and onion in the olive oil over medium heat for 15 minutes, or until the onion is translucent. Add the sausage, garlic, fennel seeds, and thyme; cook until the fennel is caramelized and the sausage is just underdone, about 10 minutes. Cool to room temperature, then refrigerate the filling until needed for assembling the focaccia.

To prepare the stuffed focaccia: Preheat the oven to 450°F. Lightly oil a 10-inch-round by 3-inch-high ring mold and line a sheet pan with parchment paper. Place the ring mold on the sheet pan and sprinkle the bottom with cornmeal. Carefully transfer half of the focaccia dough into the bottom of the ring mold; press it gently to cover the bottom of the mold. Spoon half of the filling over the dough and cover with the remaining focaccia dough. Brush the top of the dough with olive oil and spoon the remaining filling over the dough. Bake the focaccia for 10 minutes, opening the oven three times at even intervals to spray the interior walls with water to create steam. Lower the heat to 400°F and bake for an additional 35 minutes, or until light golden brown. Cool the focaccia slightly before removing the mold. Cut into wedges and serve.

WINE NOTES

This shouldn't be just a side dish—it's big enough for the whole meal! With all of the brown spice flavors from the sausage and the toasted crust, a Pinot Noir from Monterey would be a remarkable choice. The Sleepy Hollow Pinot from Barnett Vineyards has a medium- to full-bodied, spicy style that highlights the sausage and the fennel. The wine also has bright acidity, which stops the focaccia from being too heavy or opulent.

Shaved Fennel Salad with Mustard Vinaigrette and Marcona Almonds

Serves 4

This preparation is easy to put together, and its flavors are distinct and explosive. Shaved fennel, Belgian endive, Asian pear, and Marcona almonds blend seamlessly to create a poetic combination of flavors. Baby greens and tomatoes provide clean notes that form a backdrop for the other, more assertive ingredients. The thread that weaves all the components together is the whole grain mustard vinaigrette, with its elegant bite. Try serving this salad before a meat or fish entrée, or simply place a grilled chicken breast or a piece of poached fish on top of the mixture for an ideal light summer meal.

MUSTARD VINAIGRETTE
2 tablespoons whole grain mustard
1 tablespoon apple cider vinegar
2 tablespoons water
½ cup extra virgin olive oil
Salt and freshly ground black pepper

SALAD
2 cups shaved fennel bulb
2 cups firmly packed mixed baby
  greens, cleaned
1 head Belgian endive, julienned
Salt and freshly ground black pepper

GARNISH
4 teaspoons extra virgin olive oil
½ cup halved red teardrop tomatoes
½ cup halved yellow teardrop tomatoes
1 cup small-diced peeled Asian pear
½ cup Marcona almonds, toasted
  and coarsely chopped
⅓ cup coarsely chopped fennel fronds
Freshly ground black pepper

METHOD
To prepare the vinaigrette: Place the mustard, vinegar, and water in a bowl; slowly whisk in the olive oil. Season to taste with salt and pepper.

To prepare the salad: Place the fennel, baby greens, and endive in a mixing bowl. Toss with 2 tablespoons of the mustard vinaigrette and season to taste with salt and pepper.

ASSEMBLY
Drizzle the olive oil around each plate. Spoon the mustard vinaigrette in a circle around the plate. Arrange some of the salad mixture in a high mound in the center of each plate. Sprinkle the tomatoes, pear, and almonds around the salad. Sprinkle the fennel fronds over the salad and top with pepper.

WINE NOTES
Grüner Veltliner, growing more popular as people discover its versatility and concentration of flavor, has the right texture and balance to pair with this fennel salad. Although it is the most-planted white grape in Austria, it is rarely, if ever, grown outside of that country. Loimer's "Spiegel" Grüner Veltliner from Langenlois has mineral notes and faint aromas of mustard, which make it perfect with the vinaigrette and the shaved fennel.

Roasted Duck with Prosciutto-Wrapped Fennel Bulb and Balsamic-Cherry Sauce

Serves 4

Although this roasted duck, encrusted with fennel and coriander seeds, sings with flavor, it isn't the center of attention on the plate. That honor goes to the whole roasted fennel bulb, which has been wrapped in prosciutto and caul fat. It cuts like a pat of soft butter, and the combination of lightly salty ham with the anise-flavored fennel simply monopolizes your attention. The caul fat keeps everything succulent, moist, and rich. A playful balsamic-cherry sauce fuses the flavors of the fennel and duck together. Almost any roasted meat would stand in nicely for the duck. Or you could serve the fennel by itself—your guests will be stunned.

FENNEL BULBS

2 large fennel bulbs, tops trimmed
Freshly ground black pepper
1 pound prosciutto, thinly sliced
¼ pound caul fat
1 tablespoon grapeseed oil
8 sprigs thyme
4 bay leaves

DUCK

1 fresh duck
Salt and freshly ground black pepper
2 sprigs sage
1 sprig rosemary
3 tablespoons fennel seeds,
   toasted and crushed
1 tablespoon coriander seeds,
   toasted and crushed

BALSAMIC-CHERRY SAUCE

½ cup chopped dried sweet cherries
1 tablespoon balsamic vinegar
½ cup pan juices from fennel (above)
Freshly ground black pepper

GARNISH

2 tablespoons coarsely chopped
   fennel fronds
1 teaspoon crushed coriander seeds
Freshly ground black pepper
8 teaspoons Fennel Oil *(see Appendices)*

METHOD

To prepare the fennel bulbs: Season the fennel bulbs with pepper. Wrap each bulb in ½ pound of prosciutto, then wrap tightly with the caul fat. Wrap tightly in plastic wrap and refrigerate for 30 minutes. Preheat the oven to 325°F. Place the grapeseed oil in an ovenproof sauté pan and heat to medium-high heat. Remove the plastic wrap and sear the fennel bulbs in the oil on all sides until golden brown, 3 to 4 minutes on each side. Add the thyme and bay leaves; roast in the oven for 2 hours, or until the fennel bulbs are tender, turning them periodically while cooking. Reserve ½ cup of the pan juices for making the reduction. Allow the fennel bulbs to rest for 5 minutes before slicing in half and then into wedges.

To prepare the duck: Preheat the oven to 425°F. Season the cavity of the duck and the skin with salt and pepper. Stuff the sage and rosemary inside the cavity of the duck. Rub the outside of the duck with the fennel and coriander seeds. Place the duck on a rack set in a roasting pan and bake for 7 minutes. Reduce the heat to 375°F and roast for 1 hour, or until the duck is cooked to medium. Allow the duck to rest for 15 minutes before carving. Cut the duck breasts off the bone and slice the breasts into ½-inch-thick pieces. If you like, you can serve the duck legs; alternately, reserve them for another use.

To prepare the sauce: Place the cherries, vinegar, and reserved pan juices in a small saucepan; whisk to combine. Warm over medium heat until hot and season to taste with pepper.

ASSEMBLY

Place a few slices of the roasted fennel bulb on each plate and arrange the duck meat in front. Spoon the sauce over the duck and around the plate. Sprinkle the fennel fronds and coriander around the plate and top with pepper. Drizzle the Fennel Oil around the duck and fennel bulb.

WINE NOTES

The Douro Valley of Portugal is generally known for its fortified wines, or Ports. Quinta das Tecedeiras "Reserva" utilizes the same grapes as Port but is made into a dry, unfortified red wine. The brown, caramelized flavors of the prosciutto and the essence of the cherries are echoed in the black cherry and spice notes of the Tecedeiras. The bright acidity of the Port also makes an ideal contrast to the richness of the roasted duck.

Smoked Chicken and Fennel Terrine with Fennel Purée

Serves 8

*One of chicken's greatest friends is fennel, as this gorgeous and sophisticated terrine demonstrates.
It would kick off a special dinner party with a dramatic statement. Cubes of fennel and smoked chicken are suspended
in a delicate gelée, and a fennel and apple salad and fennel purée ensure that this preparation is a
love note to this most regal of vegetables. As an alternative, try lobster or shrimp in place of the chicken.*

TERRINE

2 fennel bulbs, tops trimmed
3 skinless, boneless chicken breasts
Salt and freshly ground black pepper
1 tablespoon grapeseed oil
2 cups dry hickory chips plus 1 cup
   hickory chips soaked overnight in water
   to cover, then drained
2 cups Fennel Stock or Vegetable Stock
   (see Appendices)
8 sheets gelatin, bloomed
¼ cup chopped fennel fronds
1 cup Pickled Red Onion *(see Appendices)*,
   drained

APPLE-FENNEL SALAD

1 cup shaved fennel bulb
3 red radishes, julienned
½ cup julienned Granny Smith apple
2 teaspoons freshly squeezed lemon juice
1 tablespoon extra virgin olive oil
Salt and freshly ground black pepper

FENNEL PURÉE

½ cup chopped fennel fronds
¼ cup chopped fennel bulb
¼ cup extra virgin olive oil
½ teaspoon minced garlic
3 tablespoons cold water
2 teaspoons freshly squeezed lemon juice
Salt and freshly ground black pepper

GARNISH

8 micro breakfast radishes
2 tablespoons Fennel Oil *(see Appendices)*
¼ cup micro parsley sprouts (or chopped
   fresh flat-leaf parsley)
Freshly ground black pepper

METHOD

To prepare the terrine: Preheat the oven to 350°F. Wrap the fennel bulbs in aluminum foil and place in an ovenproof pan. Roast the fennel for 1 hour, or until tender. Cool the fennel to room temperature and cut into medium dice.

Prepare a medium-hot grill. Season the chicken with salt and pepper and brush with the grapeseed oil. Place the dry hickory chips over the hot coals in the grill. When the dry chips catch fire, sprinkle the wet chips over the coals. Place the chicken breasts on the grill and cover tightly with the grill lid. Smoke for 7 minutes. Turn the breasts over and smoke for 5 to 7 minutes longer, or until the chicken is cooked. Remove the chicken from the grill and cut into medium dice. Season to taste with salt and pepper.

Warm the stock in a saucepan and remove from the heat. Add the gelatin and fennel fronds. Line an 8-inch-long by 1½-inch-wide by 2¼-inch-high terrine mold with plastic wrap. In a mixing bowl, toss the diced fennel and chicken, the pickled onion, and the gelatin mixture to combine. Spoon the mixture into the terrine mold, draining off any excess gelatin liquid. Fill the terrine mold to the top and cover with plastic wrap. Refrigerate the terrine overnight, or until firm. Remove the terrine from the mold and tighten the plastic wrap around it. Cut the terrine into ½-inch-thick slices, and only then carefully peel away the plastic wrap from each slice. Season each slice with salt and pepper.

To prepare the salad: Toss the fennel, radishes, apple, lemon juice, and olive oil together in a bowl. Season to taste with salt and pepper.

To prepare the fennel purée: Just before serving, place the fennel fronds, fennel bulb, olive oil, garlic, water, and lemon juice in a blender; purée until smooth. Pass through a fine-mesh sieve if fibrous and season to taste with salt and pepper. Use as soon as possible; the bright green color can fade if it sits too long.

ASSEMBLY

Place a slice of the terrine in the center of each plate, on an angle. Place a small mound of the apple-fennel salad at 12 o'clock and 2 of the micro breakfast radishes at 2 o'clock. Spoon the fennel purée and Fennel Oil around the plate and sprinkle with the micro parsley sprouts. Top with pepper.

WINE NOTES

Although smoked chicken may seem like red wine territory, the green fennel frond purée makes this dish more white wine friendly. Aged Châteauneuf-du-Pape *blanc* is a rarity (about 95 percent of Châteauneufs are red), but its smoky, mineral flavors and high tones of apple are delicious. When paired with this terrine, those flavors are accented and the fennel recedes to an elegant background for the dish.

GREENS

Mille-Feuille with Spinach, Caper Berries, and Tomato Vinaigrette

Serves 6

This would be a superb first course for a celebration dinner. Oven-roasted tomatoes and creamy ricotta cheese are ideal supporting components for the garlic-flavored stewed spinach. All the ingredients are magnificently contained between layers of buttery and crispy puff pastry. A balsamic-tinged vinaigrette, caper berries, and tiny herbs round out this starter with whimsical flavor notes. To take it to another level, try layering slices of smoked salmon into the mille-feuille.

OVEN-ROASTED TOMATOES

8 tomatoes
1½ tablespoons extra virgin olive oil
1½ teaspoons chopped fresh thyme
Salt and freshly ground black pepper

SPINACH

3 cups firmly packed spinach leaves,
   blanched
2 tablespoons extra virgin olive oil
¼ cup minced shallot
1 tablespoon minced garlic
Salt and freshly ground black pepper

RICOTTA

1 cup ricotta cheese
2 tablespoons extra virgin olive oil
2 teaspoons white wine vinegar
2 tablespoons chopped fresh chives
Salt and freshly ground black pepper

VINAIGRETTE

3 tablespoons cooked spinach (above)
2 tablespoons brunoise-cut red tomato
1 tablespoon tomato juice
2 tablespoons balsamic vinegar
⅛ teaspoon minced garlic
¼ cup extra virgin olive oil
Salt and freshly ground black pepper

4 ¼-inch-thick pieces of puff pastry,
   each about 6 by 8 inches

GARNISH

12 caper berries, thinly sliced
6 teaspoons chiffonade-cut fresh basil
6 teaspoons micro herbs (or chopped
   fresh herbs)
Freshly ground black pepper
6 teaspoons Herb Oil *(see Appendices)*

METHOD

To prepare the tomatoes: Preheat the oven to 275˚F. Blanch the tomatoes in boiling salted water for 1 minute to loosen the skin. Remove their skins, quarter the tomatoes, and remove the seeds and ribs. This yields 32 pieces of tomato that resemble tulip petals. Lay the tomato petals on a rack-lined sheet pan. Lightly brush the petals with the olive oil; sprinkle with the thyme. Roast in the oven for 30 minutes, then pat dry with a towel. Season with salt and pepper.

To prepare the spinach: Squeeze any excess liquid from the spinach and coarsely chop. Heat the olive oil in a sauté pan over medium heat. Sweat the shallot and garlic in the pan until translucent, about 2 minutes. Add the spinach and cook for 3 minutes. Season to taste with salt and pepper and cool to room temperature; reserve 3 tablespoons of the cooked spinach for the vinaigrette.

To prepare the ricotta: Combine the ricotta, olive oil, vinegar, and chives in a mixing bowl; season to taste with salt and pepper. Refrigerate until needed.

To prepare the vinaigrette: Combine the 3 tablespoons cooked spinach, the tomato, tomato juice, vinegar, and garlic in a small bowl; slowly whisk in the olive oil. Season to taste with salt and pepper.

To prepare the mille-feuille: Preheat the oven to 315˚F. Line a sheet pan with parchment paper. Lay the puff pastry slices on the prepared pan. Place a piece of parchment paper on top of the pastry and set another sheet pan on top, leaving a little bit of room between the sheet pans (you can lay a knife at the two ends of the sheet pans). Bake for 25 to 30 minutes, or until golden brown.

Place a piece of the puff pastry on a smooth work surface. Spread a thin layer of the ricotta over the puff pastry, then a layer of the tomato and a layer of the spinach. Add a second layer of ricotta. Repeat the process with the puff pastry, ricotta, tomato, and spinach to make 3 layers of filling. Top with a final layer of the puff pastry. Slice the mille-feuille with a very sharp knife into 1-inch-thick slices.

ASSEMBLY

Carefully transfer 1 slice to each plate. Spoon the vinaigrette around the mille-feuille. Arrange the caper berries, basil, and micro herbs around the plate and top with pepper. Drizzle the Herb Oil around the mille-feuille.

WINE NOTES

A cool-climate Chardonnay that has seen contact with oak is able to adjust to the green flavors of the spinach and the richness of the ricotta cheese. Château de la Maltroye's *premier cru* Chassagne-Montrachet is able to focus these ingredients and complement the buttery toastiness of the puff pastry. The Maltroye also holds up against the sharp acid accent of the caper berries, which causes many wines to seem disjointed and flabby.

Lamb with Stir-Fried Tatsoi, Mizuna, Julienned Vegetables, and Spicy Peanut Sauce

Serves 4

Here succulent slices of lamb tenderloin are spread out on an explosively flavored bed of stir-fried vegetables and greens. A spicy, velvety peanut sauce is drizzled around the plate to weave the meat and vegetables gloriously together. As a fun alternative, try substituting portobello or shiitake mushrooms for the lamb—you will be hard-pressed to discover a more flavorful vegetarian preparation.

LAMB

1½ pounds lamb tenderloin
¼ cup sesame oil
2 cloves garlic, minced
2 tablespoons sansho or Szechuan
  peppercorns, crushed
Salt

SPICY PEANUT SAUCE

2 cups unsalted peanuts in shells
1 tablespoon sesame oil
1 tablespoon coconut oil
1 tablespoon minced fresh ginger
½ jalapeño chile, seeded and chopped
1 red Thai chile, seeded and chopped
1½ tablespoons soy sauce
1½ tablespoons rice wine vinegar
1 tablespoon chopped fresh cilantro
2 tablespoons grapeseed oil
About ½ cup water
Salt and freshly ground black pepper

STIR-FRY

1½ tablespoons sesame oil
2 tablespoons minced fresh ginger
1 tablespoon minced garlic
4 scallions, cut diagonally into thin slices
½ cup julienned red onion
1 carrot, peeled and julienned
1 parsnip, peeled and julienned
1 yellow bell pepper, julienned
1 red bell pepper, julienned
1 cup shredded red cabbage
2 tablespoons sesame seeds
3 cups loosely packed tatsoi
3 cups loosely packed mizuna
Salt and freshly ground black pepper

GARNISH

4 teaspoons toasted sesame oil
4 tablespoons micro opal basil
  (or chopped opal basil leaves)

METHOD

To prepare the lamb: Coat the lamb with the sesame oil and rub with the garlic and peppercorns. Refrigerate the lamb for 1 hour before cooking. Preheat a sauté pan over high heat. Season the lamb with salt and add to the pan. Cook for 5 to 7 minutes on each side, or until medium-rare. Remove from the pan and let rest for 3 minutes before slicing thinly.

To prepare the peanut sauce: Shell the peanuts. Place the peanuts, sesame oil, coconut oil, ginger, chiles, soy sauce, vinegar, cilantro, and grapeseed oil in a blender and purée until smooth. Add the water as necessary to create a thick, saucelike consistency. Season to taste with salt and pepper. Heat the sauce just prior to use.

To prepare the stir-fry: Preheat a wok over high heat. Add the sesame oil, ginger, garlic, and scallions; stir-fry for 1 minute. Add the red onion, carrot, and parsnip; stir-fry for 2 minutes. Add the bell peppers, cabbage, and sesame seeds; continue to cook for 3 more minutes, or until all the vegetables are tender. Add the tatsoi and mizuna; cook for 1 minute, just until the greens are wilted. Season to taste with salt and pepper.

ASSEMBLY

Arrange some of the stir-fry in a line across each plate. Lay lamb slices atop the stir-fry. Spoon the spicy peanut sauce and toasted sesame oil around the plate. Sprinkle with the micro opal basil.

WINE NOTES

Most people would think matching a German Riesling with lamb would be cause for firing the sommelier! But in this particular dish, the lamb is not the most important element of the preparation; instead, the peanut sauce and the stir-fried vegetables direct the choice to the Riesling Auslese from Franz Künstler in the Rheingau. The spicy peanut sauce causes red wines to taste hot and alcoholic, whereas the moderate level of sweetness in the Riesling tones down the heat of the chiles.

Sorrel Soup with Scallops, Grapefruit, and Grilled Scallions and Rhubarb

Serves 4

The tastes and textures of this dish combine to achieve a very special result.
The sorrel soup has a clean flavor and an assertive citrus bite that showcases the full-flavored scallops.
Rhubarb, scallions, and grapefruit provide additional notes. The blend
of familiar tastes paradoxically results in an eating experience that is strikingly different.

SORREL SOUP
3 cups firmly packed sorrel, cleaned
1 cup firmly packed spinach leaves,
    blanched
3 cups water
1 green apple, chopped
3 tablespoons extra virgin olive oil
2 tablespoons freshly squeezed lemon juice
Salt and freshly ground black pepper

SCALLOPS
4 large sea scallops
Salt and freshly ground black pepper
2 teaspoons grapeseed oil

SCALLIONS AND RHUBARB
8 scallions, cut into thirds
2 stalks rhubarb, cut into 3-inch-long by
    ⅛-inch-thick pieces
1 tablespoon grapeseed oil

GARNISH
¼ cup brunoise-cut green apple
Salt and freshly ground black pepper
1 cup small bite-size wedges daikon
½ cup water
1 tablespoon freshly squeezed lemon juice
8 grapefruit segments, supremed,
    each cut into thirds
Freshly ground black pepper

METHOD
To prepare the soup: Place the sorrel, spinach, water, apple, olive oil, and lemon juice in a blender and purée until smooth. Pass through a fine-mesh sieve. Heat the soup just prior to serving and season to taste with salt and pepper.

To prepare the scallops: Prepare a medium-hot grill. Season the scallops with salt and pepper and brush with the grapeseed oil. Place the scallops on the grill and grill for 2 to 3 minutes on each side, or until just cooked through.

To prepare the scallions and rhubarb: Rub the scallions and rhubarb with the grapeseed oil and grill for 1 to 2 minutes on each side, or until tender. Chop 4 pieces of scallion and 4 pieces of rhubarb into small dice and reserve for the garnish.

To prepare the garnish: Combine the apple with the reserved diced scallions and rhubarb and season to taste with salt and pepper. Place the daikon, water, and lemon juice in a small saucepan and bring to a simmer. Cook the daikon for 5 minutes, or until it is tender yet still crunchy.

ASSEMBLY
Ladle the soup into the center of each shallow serving bowl. Arrange some of the grapefruit and daikon pieces in the center of the soup. Place some of the scallion and rhubarb pieces over the daikon and grapefruit. Carefully coat each scallop with the apple mixture. Set a scallop in the center of each bowl and top with pepper.

WINE NOTES
The multiple layers of tastes here are stunning. A successful match requires the wine to change like a chameleon, at once withstanding the assault of the high-acid soup, the sweet-tart apples, and the mineral flavor of the scallops, while not overpowering the subtle notes added by grapefruit and rhubarb. A Riesling Kabinett from the Mosel overcomes all of these challenges with its combination of delicate sweetness, crisp acid, and light body. Fritz Haag and Selbach-Oster produce thrilling examples.

Rabbit with Wilted Arugula Salad, Figs, and Goat Cheese

Serves 4

This preparation is rife with invigorating tastes. The wilted arugula is spicy, cutting into the lean, delicately flavored rabbit loin. Voluptuous sweet fig tames and balances the arugula. Whipped goat cheese provides a welcome creaminess without making the overall combination too rich. Best of all, the whole dish takes only minutes to prepare. Serve it as a small first course or increase the portion size to make it a complete meal.

ARUGULA PURÉE
1½ cups loosely packed arugula leaves
1 cup firmly packed spinach leaves
2 tablespoons extra virgin olive oil
2 tablespoons water
Salt and freshly ground black pepper

RABBIT AND ARUGULA SALAD
1 tablespoon grapeseed oil
4 rabbit tenderloins
Salt and freshly ground black pepper
1 tablespoon extra virgin olive oil
¼ cup julienned yellow onion
⅛ teaspoon minced garlic
4 fresh figs, cut into sixths
2 cups firmly packed arugula leaves
1 tablespoon balsamic vinegar
2 tablespoons chopped walnuts

GOAT CHEESE
½ cup soft fresh goat cheese
1 tablespoon minced shallot
1½ tablespoons heavy whipping cream
Salt and freshly ground black pepper

GARNISH
4 teaspoons extra virgin olive oil
2 tablespoons chopped opal basil
Freshly ground black pepper

METHOD

To prepare the arugula purée: Place the arugula, spinach, olive oil, and water in a blender and purée until smooth. Season to taste with salt and pepper. Warm slightly just prior to serving.

To prepare the rabbit and arugula salad: Head the grapeseed oil in a sauté pan over high heat. Season the rabbit with salt and pepper and add to the pan. Cook for 2 minutes on each side, or until just cooked through. Remove from the pan, let rest 2 minutes, and then slice thinly on the diagonal. Add the olive oil, onion, and garlic to the same pan and sauté over high heat for 2 minutes, or until the onion is translucent. Add the figs and cook for 2 more minutes. Add the arugula, vinegar, and walnuts; cook just until the arugula is wilted. Season to taste with salt and pepper. Drain and reserve any juices that remain in the pan.

To prepare the goat cheese: Combine the goat cheese, shallot, and cream in a mixing bowl until smooth. Season to taste with salt and pepper. Shape into 4 quenelle-shaped pieces.

ASSEMBLY

Spoon some of the warmed arugula purée in a triangle shape on each plate. Arrange some of the rabbit and the arugula salad in the center of the triangle. Place a quenelle of the goat cheese at the base of the rabbit. Spoon some arugula salad over the rabbit. Drizzle the reserved cooking juices and the olive oil around the plate. Sprinkle with the opal basil and top with pepper.

WINE NOTES

Theoretically, a Sauvignon Blanc would be the ultimate combination with the goat cheese and the green flavors of the arugula salad. In practice, though, the touch of sweetness from the figs causes Sauvignon Blanc to taste thin and overly tart. It came as a shock that the top wine for this dish is a Bourgogne *rouge* from Robert Groffier. In contrast to a Sauvignon Blanc, the red cherry and fruit aromas of the Bourgogne *rouge* marry with the figs, while the wine still retains enough acidity to match the goat cheese and the wilted arugula.

Monkfish with Warm Endive, Apple, and Onion Salad and Watercress Purée

Serves 4

*Meaty monkfish sits on a lighthearted mixture of endive, apple, and wilted watercress;
then the peppery taste of the watercress is divinely reprised in a satiny puréed sauce.
With its clean and simple but very satisfying flavors, this dish can be served as a light main course
or, in smaller portions, as the perfect appetizer before a roasted meat entrée.*

WATERCRESS PURÉE

2 cups loosely packed watercress leaves
½ cup firmly packed spinach leaves
1 clove garlic, minced
½ cup coarsely chopped walnuts
½ cup extra virgin olive oil
2 tablespoons freshly squeezed lime juice
½ cup water
Salt and freshly ground black pepper

MONKFISH

2 teaspoons grapeseed oil
1½ pounds bone-in monkfish
Salt and freshly ground black pepper
1 teaspoon butter
1 tablespoon plus 1 teaspoon freshly
    squeezed lemon juice
1 head Belgian endive, julienned
1 red apple, julienned
½ cup julienned red onion
2 tablespoons extra virgin olive oil
1 tablespoon freshly squeezed orange juice
2 cups loosely packed watercress, thick
    stems discarded
Salt and freshly ground black pepper

GARNISH

2 tablespoons micro herbs (or chopped
    fresh herbs)
Freshly ground black pepper

METHOD

To prepare the watercress purée: Place the watercress, spinach, garlic, walnuts, olive oil, lime juice, and water in a blender and purée until smooth. Pass through a fine-mesh sieve if stringy. Season to taste with salt and pepper. Warm the purée just prior to use, but be careful not to overheat as the color will fade.

To prepare the monkfish: Heat the grapeseed oil in a sauté pan over high heat. Season the monkfish with salt and pepper and add to the pan. Sauté the monkfish for 5 to 7 minutes on each side, adding the butter halfway through. Once the monkfish is golden brown, drizzle the 1 teaspoon lemon juice over it. Remove from the pan and let rest for 3 minutes before boning and thinly slicing into 24 slices. Add the endive, apple, onion, and olive oil to the same pan. Sauté for 5 minutes; add the 1 tablespoon lemon juice and the orange juice and continue to cook for 2 minutes. Once the vegetables are tender, add the watercress and cook just until the watercress is wilted. Season to taste with salt and pepper.

ASSEMBLY

Cover the bottom of each plate with a thin layer of the warmed purée. Arrange some of the apple-vegetable mixture in a mound in the center of the purée. Place 6 slices of the monkfish around the purée and sprinkle with the micro herbs. Top with pepper.

WINE NOTES

The watercress and green flavors seem to make a light crisp Sauvignon Blanc with grassy notes an ideal pairing here. In actuality, these wines become astringent and harsh even while they reflect some of the flavors. A Condrieu from Tardieu-Laurent and a Hermitage *blanc* from Domaine des Remizières both harmonize with the monkfish even though they do not echo all of the elements in the dish. Their full-bodied, round, and smooth textures emphasize that in wine and food pairing, the proper structure is of supreme importance, while flavor is of secondary significance.

Ivory Salmon with Napa Cabbage Rolls, Braised Cabbage, and Caraway Vinaigrette

Serves 4

Earthy and comforting elements combine here to make a delightfully elegant entrée.
The Napa cabbage rolls contain a mixture of potato and bacon accented with garlic and herbs. A piece of fish
in this case indulgently rich white salmon — is served alongside the rolls on a little mound of braised cabbage
that is highlighted with celery root, red onion, and apple. Finally, a drizzle of caraway vinaigrette rounds things out
with a distinctive aromatic note. Pork or lamb would make fine substitutions for the fish.

NAPA CABBAGE ROLLS

1½ cups medium-diced Yukon
  Gold potatoes
¼ cup bacon lardoons
1 shallot, minced
2 cloves garlic, minced
2 fresh sage leaves, chopped
3 sprigs thyme, stems removed
2 tablespoons chopped fresh
  flat-leaf parsley
2 tablespoons extra virgin olive oil
Balsamic vinegar
Salt and freshly ground black pepper
4 large leaves Napa cabbage, blanched
  and thick stem cores trimmed

CARAWAY VINAIGRETTE

1 tablespoon caraway seeds, toasted
  and crushed
2½ tablespoons sherry wine vinegar
½ cup extra virgin olive oil
Salt and freshly ground black pepper

BRAISED CABBAGE

¼ cup bacon lardons
2 cloves garlic, minced
2 shallots, minced
6 leaves Napa cabbage, shredded
1 cup julienned celery root
½ cup julienned red onion
½ cup julienned red apple
¾ cup Vegetable Stock (see Appendices)
2 tablespoons caraway vinaigrette (above)
Rice wine vinegar
Salt and freshly ground black pepper

IVORY SALMON

2 teaspoons grapeseed oil
4 4-ounce ivory salmon fillets, skin off
Salt and freshly ground black pepper
1 teaspoon butter

GARNISH

4 teaspoons chopped micro spinach
  (or chopped spinach leaves)

METHOD

To prepare the cabbage rolls: Cook the potatoes in boiling salted water until tender. Drain the potatoes and set aside. Render the bacon in a sauté pan; add the shallot and garlic and cook for 2 minutes. Add the sage, thyme, and parsley. Fold in the potatoes and add the olive oil. Season to taste with the vinegar, salt, and pepper. Lay a blanched Napa cabbage leaf on a bamboo maki roller, vein side up. Blot off any excess moisture. Spoon some of the potato mixture across the bottom of the leaf and carefully roll up to a thick cigarlike shape. Repeat with the remaining cabbage leaves and potato mixture. Cut each roll into two 2-inch-long pieces.

To prepare the vinaigrette: Place the caraway seeds and vinegar in a small bowl and slowly whisk in the olive oil. Season to taste with salt and pepper.

To prepare the braised cabbage: Render the bacon in a sauté pan over medium heat, about 3 minutes. Add the garlic and shallots; cook for 2 minutes. Add the cabbage and cook for 3 minutes. Add the celery root, onion, apple, and stock; simmer over medium-low heat until the cabbage and celery root are tender, about 10 minutes. Add the vinaigrette and season the cabbage mixture to taste with the vinegar, salt, and pepper.

To prepare the salmon: Heat the grapeseed oil in a sauté pan over high heat. Season the salmon with salt and pepper and add to the pan. Cook for 3 minutes; add the butter and flip over the salmon. Continue to cook for 2 to 3 minutes, or until the salmon is cooked to medium.

ASSEMBLY

Stand 2 cabbage roll pieces upright on the left side of each plate. Spoon some of the cabbage mixture into the center of the plate and top with a piece of salmon. Drizzle the vinaigrette over the salmon and around the plate. Sprinkle with the chopped micro spinach.

WINE NOTES

In Oregon, salmon and Pinot Noir go hand in hand, and when tasting this course with versions from the Willamette Valley, it is easy to see why. The Eyrie Vineyards produces an earthy example of the varietal that highlights the bacon and the spice notes of the caraway vinaigrette. Produced by David Lett, the pioneer of Oregon Pinot, Eyrie's Pinot Noir boasts a bright acidity that cuts deftly through the fattiness of the salmon and bacon.

LEGUMES

Cassoulet with Lobster, Clams, Andouille Sausage, and Cannellini Beans

Serves 4

Lobster and clams are highlighted here rather than the usual duck or lamb, and the result is refreshing. All the flavors meld into a most comforting and soothing main course. It can be prepared as one large dish, served up family style, or as described below, in individual ramekins. You can put it together ahead of time, then just pop it in the oven forty-five minutes before the dinner hour. Serve it up with a big green salad on the side.

CLAMS

½ cup diagonally sliced celery
1 cup medium-diced yellow onion
1 carrot, peeled and cut into medium dice
1 clove garlic, smashed
½ pound smoked ham hock
2 teaspoons grapeseed oil
2 cups Shellfish Stock *(see Appendices)*
½ cup white wine
20 mahogany clams, cleaned
20 Manila clams, cleaned

BEANS

2 2-inch-thick pieces bacon, cut into
    1-inch-long pieces
½ cup large-diced carrot
½ cup large-diced celery
1 cup large-diced yellow onion
2 cloves garlic, smashed
1 cup cannellini beans, soaked in water
    overnight and drained
1 cup water
2 tablespoons butter
Salt and freshly ground black pepper

2 lobster tails, cooked and sliced into
    ¼-inch-thick medallions
2 andouille sausages, halved, sliced
    diagonally, and cooked
2 tablespoons freshly squeezed
    lemon juice
2 cups brioche breadcrumbs
½ cup chopped fresh flat-leaf parsley

METHOD

To prepare the clams: In a large sauté pan over medium-high heat, cook the celery, onion, carrot, garlic, and ham hock in the grapeseed oil until caramelized, about 7 minutes. Add the stock and wine and bring to a simmer. Add the clams; cover the pan and cook for 2 to 3 minutes, or until the clams have opened (discard any clams that do not open). Remove the clams from their shells and reserve the cooking liquid. Remove the skin and bones from the ham hock and cut the meat into a small dice. Cover and reserve the clams, ham hock, and cooking liquid separately in the refrigerator.

To prepare the beans: Render the fat from the bacon in a saucepan over medium heat, about 7 minutes. Add the carrot, celery, and onion; cook until caramelized, about 7 minutes. Add the garlic, beans, water, butter, and two-thirds of the reserved clam cooking liquid. Bring to a slow simmer and cook over low heat for 2 hours, or until the beans are very tender. Pick out and discard the bacon and vegetables. Drain off any excess liquid and season the beans to taste with salt and pepper.

To prepare the cassoulet: Preheat the oven to 325°F. Lightly butter four 5-inch-diameter ramekins or small cast-iron crocks. In a large bowl or pot, combine the clams, diced ham hock, bean mixture, lobster, sausages, lemon juice, and the remaining one-third clam cooking liquid. In a separate bowl, combine the breadcrumbs and parsley. Fold half of the breadcrumb mixture into the beans. Fill the prepared ramekins or crocks with the cassoulet and sprinkle a heavy layer of the remaining breadcrumbs over the top. Bake for 45 minutes, or until the breadcrumbs are golden brown and the cassoulet is heated through. Serve immediately.

WINE NOTES

It's difficult to choose a wine that doesn't overpower the delicate seafood in this cassoulet but is still able to withstand the power of the ham hock and andouille sausages. Red Burgundies are magical with the legumes and shellfish but are overwhelmed by the spicy sausage. White wines are dominated as well. A perfect balance is found with Chapoutier's "La Bernardine" from Châteauneuf-du-Pape.

Four-Bean Venison Chili
with Black Diamond White Cheddar

Serves 4

*There are so many different ways to make chili, it's hard to know where to begin,
but this version certainly elevates the all-American favorite. For variety, four types of beans are used,
and venison is substituted for beef. A creamy white Cheddar cheese is grated over the top just prior to serving.
As with most chilis, this one is even better on day two or three. Turkey or chicken can be used instead of venison.
For a fuller flavor, try cooking the beans in chicken stock rather than water.*

BLACK TURTLE BEANS

¼ cup chopped yellow onion
1 tablespoon butter
½ cup black turtle beans, soaked
 in water overnight and drained
1 tablespoon cumin seeds
2 cups water
Salt and freshly ground black pepper

PINTO BEANS

¼ cup chopped yellow onion
1 tablespoon butter
½ cup pinto beans, soaked in water
 overnight and drained
2 jalapeño chiles, halved
2 cups water
Salt and freshly ground black pepper

GREAT NORTHERN BEANS

¼ cup chopped yellow onion
1 tablespoon butter
½ cup Great Northern beans, soaked
 in water overnight and drained
2 dried chipotle chiles
2 cups water
Salt and freshly ground black pepper

RICE BEANS

¼ cup chopped yellow onion
1 tablespoon butter
½ cup rice beans, soaked in water
 overnight and drained
¼ cup loosely packed fresh cilantro leaves
2 cups water
Salt and freshly ground black pepper

METHOD

To prepare the black turtle beans: In a medium saucepan over medium-high heat, sauté the onion in the butter until translucent, about 5 minutes. Add the beans, cumin, and water; bring to a slow simmer. Cook the beans over low heat for 2 hours, or until tender. Drain any excess liquid into a bowl, reserve the beans and liquid separately, and season to taste with salt and pepper.

To prepare the pinto beans: In another medium saucepan, sauté the onion in the butter until translucent. Add the beans, jalapeños, and water; bring to a slow simmer. Cook the beans over low heat for 2 hours, or until tender. Discard the jalapeños. Drain any excess liquid into a bowl, reserve the beans and liquid separately, and season to taste with salt and pepper.

To prepare the Great Northern beans: In another medium saucepan, sauté the onion in the butter until translucent. Add the beans, chipotles, and water; bring to a slow simmer. Cook the beans over low heat for 2 hours, or until tender. Discard the chipotles. Drain any excess liquid into a bowl, reserve the beans and liquid separately, and season to taste with salt and pepper.

To prepare the rice beans: In another medium saucepan, sauté the onion in the butter until translucent. Add the beans, cilantro, and water; bring to a slow simmer. Cook the beans over low heat for 2 hours, or until tender. Drain any excess liquid into a bowl, reserve the beans and liquid separately, and season to taste with salt and pepper.

Four-Bean Venison Chili with Black Diamond White Cheddar

CHILI
2½ pounds ground venison
2 cloves garlic, minced
1½ cups small-diced red onion
1 ancho chile, soaked in warm water
    and chopped
¼ cup chili powder
½ cup tomato paste
3 large tomatoes, diced
3 juniper berries, finely crushed
2 bay leaves
3 tablespoons cumin seeds, crushed
1½ tablespoons red wine vinegar
4 ounces bittersweet chocolate, chopped
2 cups bean cooking liquid (above)
Salt and freshly ground black pepper

GARNISH
1½ cups grated Black Diamond white
    Cheddar
¼ cup minced red onion
¼ cup chiffonade-cut fresh cilantro
⅓ cup chopped scallion tops

To prepare the chili: In a large saucepan over medium-high heat, brown the ground venison with the garlic and onion, about 10 minutes. Drain off any excess fat and add the ancho chile, chili powder, tomato paste, tomatoes, juniper berries, bay leaves, cumin, vinegar, chocolate, and 2 cups reserved bean cooking liquid. Simmer the chili slowly for 30 minutes, or until all the flavors have melded. Season to taste with salt and pepper.

ASSEMBLY
Place spoonfuls of the beans at 4 separate points in each shallow bowl. Ladle the venison chili over the beans and sprinkle with the cheese, red onion, cilantro, and scallions.

WINE NOTES
After trying several different red wines with this chili and finding them all to be hot and alcoholic, and then tasting a few whites that were dominated by the power of the venison, I realized that my father always pairs the perfect beverage with chili—beer. Chicago's Goose Island brewery produces Honker's Ale, a pale ale that isn't overwhelmed by the venison. The lower level of alcohol works to tone down the spice of the chili as well.

Sesame Chicken with Chinese Long Bean Stir-Fry

Serves 4

Though quite simple to make, this recipe has extraordinary flavors and textures.
The beautiful thing is that once all the ingredients are prepped and ready, the entire dish takes
only minutes to assemble, so it is ideal for feeding a busy family. For a heartier version,
add mushrooms to the stir-fry, and feel free to adjust the seasonings to make it as spicy as you desire.
Lobster or salmon would make wonderful substitutions for the chicken.

CHICKEN

¼ cup toasted sesame oil
2 tablespoons minced fresh ginger
3 tablespoons soy sauce
1 tablespoon minced garlic
1 teaspoon chile oil
1 dried red Thai chile, chopped
4 small chicken breasts, skin on

STIR-FRY

¼ cup toasted sesame oil
2 cloves garlic, minced
3 tablespoons minced fresh ginger
2 cups Chinese broccoli, cleaned and cut
   into bite-size pieces
4 cups Chinese long beans, blanched
   and cut into 3-inch-long pieces
1 cup julienned red onion
1 cup bamboo shoots
3 scallions, chopped
2 tablespoons rice wine vinegar
1 tablespoon chile-garlic sauce
2 tablespoons hoisin sauce
2 tablespoons soy sauce
2 tablespoons freshly squeezed
   yuzu citron juice

GARNISH

2 tablespoons chopped fresh cilantro

METHOD

To prepare the chicken: Whisk together the sesame oil, ginger, soy sauce, garlic, chile oil, and chile. Coat the chicken with the marinade and refrigerate, covered, for 1 hour. Heat a sauté pan over medium-high heat. Add the marinade juices and the chicken, skin side down. Cook for 5 minutes, or until the skin is golden brown; turn the chicken over and continue to cook for 5 to 7 minutes longer, or until just cooked through. Remove the chicken from the pan and let rest for 3 minutes before slicing into 1-inch-thick slices.

To prepare the stir-fry: Preheat a wok over high heat. Add the sesame oil, garlic, and ginger; stir-fry for 1 minute. Add the Chinese broccoli, long beans, and onion; stir-fry for 3 minutes. Add the bamboo shoots, scallions, vinegar, chile-garlic sauce, hoisin sauce, soy sauce, and yuzu citron juice; continue to cook for 2 to 3 minutes longer, or until all the vegetables are tender.

ASSEMBLY

Place some of the stir-fry in the center of each plate and arrange the chicken slices atop the vegetables. Spoon the juices from the stir-fry over the chicken and around the plate. Sprinkle with the chopped cilantro.

WINE NOTES

Many people consider the Rheingau region of Germany the finest place to grow Riesling in the world (though the Austrians and Alsatians might disagree!). Riesling Kabinett from Balthasar Ress is an excellent example from this area; it combines skillfully with the Asian flavors in the stir-fry. Also, the hint of smooth sweetness from the wine contrasts with the spicy bite of the ginger, while the Riesling's citrus notes highlight the aromatic yuzu.

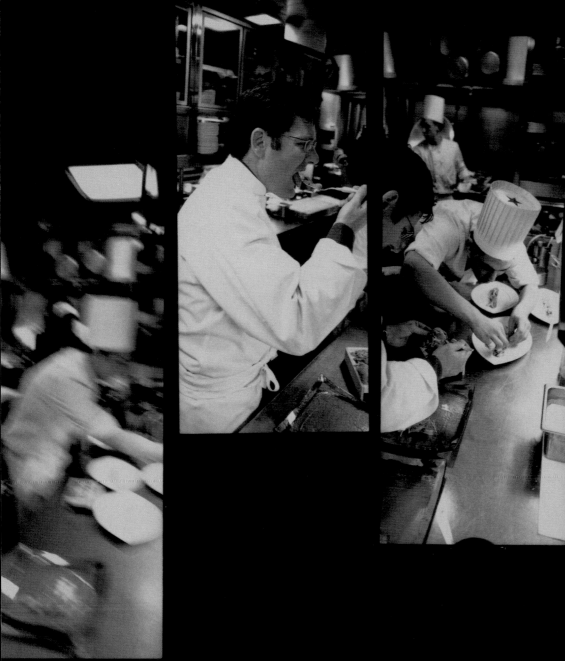

Swiss Chard and Wild Mushroom–Wrapped Cod with Cauliflower Mushroom and Edamame Sauce

Serves 4

In this preparation, the cod stays especially moist because it is covered in mushrooms and then wrapped in Swiss chard and steamed. The fish is delicate and just flakes apart, but at the same time the mushrooms provide a grounding element. Edamame sauce adds an exotic flavor and a soothing creaminess. The unusual cauliflower mushroom provides an additional earthy note and a playfully crunchy texture (though any mushroom can be substituted). Drizzles of sesame oil and soy sauce are the final flavor points that tie everything together. If desired, you can substitute chicken for the cod.

EDAMAME SAUCE

2 cups shucked edamame, blanched
¼ cup extra virgin olive oil
¼ cup grapeseed oil
¾ cup cold water
1 tablespoon freshly squeezed lime juice
Salt and freshly ground black pepper

COD

1 teaspoon minced garlic
2 teaspoons minced fresh ginger
1 tablespoon toasted sesame oil
1 cup shiitake mushrooms, thinly sliced
1 cup cremini mushrooms, thinly sliced
3 Swiss chard leaves, blanched, thick stems removed and chopped, and leaves and stems reserved separately
1 tablespoon soy sauce
1 tablespoon rice wine vinegar
1 tablespoon chile-garlic sauce
Salt and freshly ground black pepper
1 12-ounce cod fillet (about 2 inches wide)
¼ cup large chunks fresh ginger
3 1-inch pieces fresh lemongrass
½ lemon
4 sprigs flat-leaf parsley

VEGETABLES

1 tablespoon minced fresh ginger
1½ tablespoons sesame oil
1 1-pound cauliflower mushroom, cut into eighths
½ cup shucked edamame, blanched
½ cup enoki mushrooms, trimmed
2 heads baby bok choy, blanched and halved
1½ tablespoons rice wine vinegar
1 tablespoon mirin
2 tablespoons soy sauce
¼ cup hijiki seaweed, soaked in water for 1 hour and drained

4 teaspoons soy sauce
4 teaspoons toasted sesame oil
¼ cup loosely packed fresh flat-leaf parsley leaves
Freshly ground black pepper

METHOD

To prepare the sauce: Purée the edamame, olive oil, grapeseed oil, water, and lime juice in a blender until smooth. Pass through a fine-mesh sieve if fibrous and season to taste with salt and pepper. Warm the sauce gently just prior to use.

To prepare the cod: Sauté the minced garlic and ginger in the sesame oil over medium heat until translucent, about 4 minutes. Add the shiitake and cremini mushrooms and cook for 2 minutes. Add the Swiss chard stems, soy sauce, vinegar, and chile-garlic sauce; cook until the mushrooms are tender, about 5 minutes. Season to taste with salt and pepper. Chop the mushroom mixture into a fine paste. Season the cod with salt and pepper. Cover the top of the cod with the mushroom paste, then tightly wrap the cod in the blanched Swiss chard leaves. Place the ginger chunks, lemongrass, lemon, and parsley in a steamer and cover with water. Place the wrapped cod on a rack over the liquid and steam for 8 minutes. Remove and slice into 4 pieces. Season the steamed cod with salt and pepper.

To prepare the vegetables: Sauté the ginger in the sesame oil over high heat for 30 seconds. Add the cauliflower mushroom and cook for 2 minutes. Add the edamame, enoki mushrooms, bok choy, vinegar, and mirin; continue to cook until the mushrooms are tender, about 5 minutes. Add the soy sauce slowly as the vegetables begin to caramelize. Remove the cauliflower mushroom and add the hijiki to the pan.

ASSEMBLY

Spoon a solid circle of the edamame sauce into the center of each plate. Arrange some of the cauliflower mushroom and vegetables atop the sauce and place a slice of the wrapped cod balancing upright in the center of the vegetables. Drizzle the soy sauce and sesame oil around the plate and sprinkle with the parsley and pepper.

WINE NOTES

Steamed cod has a subtle taste that can easily be overshadowed by a robust wine. The wine choice must be light to medium in body and be able to harmonize with the green notes of the bok choy and edamame sauce. Seresin Sauvignon Blanc is an ideal choice. An aromatic wine from Marlborough, New Zealand, the Seresin also has a lively acidity to balance with the Asian spices in the dish.

Legumes Three Ways

Serves 4

*Here is a little study in legumes. Each preparation—the cabbage roll, the salad, and the soup—
can be served as an individual item, or they can be combined as they are here to make a fun and provocative dish.
For an interesting, tasty menu idea, serve these three distinct items sequentially; then all you would need
to finish would be the classic Japanese red bean ice cream.*

BLACK BEAN CABBAGE ROLLS

1½ cups cooked black beans
½ cup brunoise-cut bacon, cooked
2 teaspoons chopped fresh cilantro
1 teaspoon chopped fresh chives
1 jalapeño chile, seeded and minced
Salt and freshly ground black pepper
4 Napa cabbage leaves, blanched
 and thick stems trimmed
1 tablespoon butter

SNAPPER WITH WHITE BEAN SALAD

1 cup cooked cannellini beans
1 tablespoon chopped fresh flat-leaf parsley
¼ cup small-diced Braised Artichokes
 (see Appendices)
½ cup small-diced Tomato Confit
 (see Appendices)
3 cloves Roasted Garlic *(see Appendices)*
1 tablespoon extra virgin olive oil
2 teaspoons freshly squeezed lemon juice
Salt and freshly ground black pepper
2 shallots, minced
¼ cup brunoise-cut bacon
2 teaspoons grapeseed oil
4 2-ounce snapper fillet pieces, skin on

PINTO BEAN SOUP

1 cup cooked pinto beans
1½ cups Chicken Stock *(see Appendices)*
2 teaspoons balsamic vinegar
Salt and freshly ground black pepper
½ cup Braised Collard Greens
 (see Appendices)

GARNISH

¼ cup micro chervil sprouts (or chopped
 fresh flat-leaf parsley)
¼ cup micro cilantro sprouts (or chopped
 fresh cilantro)
Freshly ground black pepper

METHOD

To prepare the cabbage rolls: Purée 1 cup of the black beans in a blender or food processor with just enough water to make a smooth consistency. Reserve ½ cup of the purée. Fold together the remaining bean purée, whole beans, bacon, cilantro, chives, and chile in a bowl. Season the bean mixture to taste with salt and pepper. Place 2 of the cabbage leaves flat on a piece of plastic wrap, overlapping. Spoon half of the filling down the middle of the cabbage leaves and roll up like a cigar. Secure tightly in the plastic wrap. Repeat with the remaining 2 cabbage leaves and filling. Just prior to use, place the plastic-wrapped cabbage rolls in a bamboo steamer and steam for 3 minutes, or until hot. Using a very sharp knife, trim the edges and cut each roll into two 2-inch-long pieces. Carefully remove the plastic wrap by cutting it away with scissors.

Place the reserved bean purée and the butter in a saucepan and warm over medium heat just prior to use. Season to taste with salt and pepper; add a touch of water if it is very thick.

To prepare the snapper with white bean salad: Combine the beans, parsley, artichokes, ¼ cup of the tomato confit, the roasted garlic, olive oil, and lemon juice in a small saucepan. Warm over medium heat; season to taste with salt and pepper. Place the shallots and bacon in a sauté pan and cook over medium-high heat for 3 to 5 minutes, or until the bacon is crispy and the shallots are caramelized. Add the remaining ¼ cup tomato confit and cook for 2 minutes longer. Heat a sauté pan over high heat. Add the grapeseed oil. Season the snapper with salt and pepper and add to the pan skin side down. Cook for 2 minutes, or until the skin is golden brown and crispy. Turn the fish over and continue to cook for 1 to 2 minutes, or until just cooked through.

To prepare the soup: Purée the beans with the stock and vinegar in a blender. Season to taste with salt and pepper. Warm the soup in a saucepan and froth with a handheld blender before using. Place some of the collard greens in the bottom of 4 tiny bowls or ramekins and cover with the pinto bean soup.

ASSEMBLY

Place the soup bowl at 11 o'clock on each plate and sprinkle with some of the chervil sprouts. Spoon some of the black bean purée between 3 and 5 o'clock and place a piece of the cabbage roll atop the purée. Sprinkle with the cilantro sprouts. Spoon some of the white bean salad at 8 o'clock on each plate and place a piece of the fish atop the beans. Crust the fish with the bacon-shallot-tomato mixture. Spoon the juices from the pan that held the white beans around the plate and top with pepper.

WINE NOTES

Depending on your mood, there are two distinct directions you can take to match this elaborate preparation. To emphasize the earthiness of the legumes, use a red Burgundy from Gevrey-Chambertin, such as Domaine Fourrier. If you are feeling more adventurous, contrast those earthy components with a fruit-forward Pinot Noir from Vision Cellars; it adds a layer of cherries and berries to the flavor of the legumes without disrupting the structure of the dish.

Spring Bean Salad with Quail Eggs, Smithfield Ham, and Hazelnut Vinaigrette

Serves 4

This salad works well either plated or served family style from a platter.
It has great textures with the haricots verts, wax beans, hard-boiled quail eggs, and hazelnuts.
The whole composition is actually quite light and delicate; it makes
an ideal lunchtime meal. Try adding thin slices of grilled or roasted pork tenderloin
for a more substantial preparation.

HAZELNUT VINAIGRETTE

2½ tablespoons sherry wine vinegar
1 tablespoon minced shallot
2 tablespoons chopped toasted hazelnuts
¼ cup hazelnut oil
¼ cup grapeseed oil
Salt and freshly ground black pepper

SALAD

1 small red onion, peeled and halved
2 cups haricots verts, blanched and cut
  diagonally into 2-inch-long pieces
2 cups yellow wax beans, blanched and
  cut diagonally into 2-inch-long pieces
3 red radishes, thinly sliced
1 cup medium-diced Smithfield ham
2 tablespoons chopped toasted hazelnuts
2 teaspoons chopped fresh flat-leaf parsley
Salt and freshly ground black pepper

GARNISH

4 ½-inch-thick slices ciabatta bread, toasted
8 quail eggs, boiled, peeled, and halved
½ cup micro greens (or chopped fresh
  flat-leaf parsley and chives)
4 teaspoons Herb Oil *(see Appendices)*
Freshly ground black pepper

METHOD

To prepare the vinaigrette: Place the vinegar, shallot, and hazelnuts in a mixing bowl; slowly whisk in both oils. Season the vinaigrette to taste with salt and pepper.

To prepare the salad: Preheat the oven to 350°F. Wrap the onion in aluminum foil and roast for 1 hour, or until tender. Cool and julienne the onion. Place the onion, haricots verts, yellow wax beans, radishes, ham, hazelnuts, and parsley in a mixing bowl; toss with half of the vinaigrette and season to taste with salt and pepper.

ASSEMBLY

Place a slice of the toasted ciabatta in the center of each plate. Place some of the salad atop the ciabatta and arrange 4 quail egg halves around the plate. Sprinkle the micro greens over the salad. Spoon some of the remaining vinaigrette and the Herb Oil over the quail eggs and around the plate. Top with pepper.

WINE NOTES

Domaine Laroche Chablis provides the best of both worlds: a stony, crisp wine balanced with a touch of oak aging and tropical fruit. "Les Vaillons" Vieilles Vignes has all the components to elevate the salad to new heights. The salty Smithfield ham is counterbalanced by the fruit notes of the Chablis, while the mineral flavors are reflected in the legumes and the radishes.

Wild Mushroom Lasagna with Arugula Pesto

Serves 4

Who says you have to make lasagna the traditional way? Here mushrooms rather than tomatoes shine, with arugula pesto providing the perfect piquant accent. The result is a combination of flavors that is both earthy and heady. This is also a fine make-ahead dish: just heat up the desired portion size whenever you need it. Add shredded duck confit between the layers for an even heartier filling.

MUSHROOM FILLING

5 cups Roasted Wild Mushrooms
  (see Appendices), finely chopped
3 tablespoons balsamic vinegar
3 tablespoons extra virgin olive oil
3 tablespoons chopped fresh basil
Salt and freshly ground black pepper

RICOTTA FILLING

2 cups ricotta cheese
1 cup blanched spinach leaves, chopped
1 tablespoon balsamic vinegar
1 clove garlic, minced
Salt and freshly ground black pepper

1 pound lasagna noodles, cooked
2 cups grated pecorino Romano cheese
1 pound (2 large bunches) arugula leaves

ARUGULA PESTO

2 cups firmly packed arugula leaves
½ cup firmly packed fresh basil
2 cloves garlic, chopped
1 cup grated pecorino Romano cheese
1 cup extra virgin olive oil
½ cup pine nuts, toasted
Salt and freshly ground black pepper

GARNISH

4 teaspoons balsamic vinegar
2 tablespoons chiffonade-cut basil
¼ cup pine nuts, toasted and chopped
2 tablespoons grated pecorino
  Romano cheese

METHOD

To prepare the mushroom filling: Combine the chopped mushrooms, vinegar, olive oil, and basil. Season to taste with salt and pepper.

To prepare the ricotta filling: Combine the ricotta, spinach, vinegar, and garlic. Season to taste with salt and pepper.

To prepare the lasagna: Preheat the oven to 375°F. Lightly oil an 8-inch-square lasagna pan. Arrange a layer of the lasagna noodles on the bottom of the pan (trim the noodles as necessary to fit). Then begin layering by spreading a layer of the mushroom filling, sprinkling with some of the pecorino Romano, adding a layer of arugula leaves, and spreading some of the ricotta filling over the arugula. Top with a second layer of the lasagna noodles. Continue this process, ultimately using half of the pecorino Romano and all of the other components, to make 6 layers of pasta and 5 layers of filling. Cover with aluminum foil and bake for 45 minutes. Remove the cover and sprinkle with the remaining 1 cup pecorino Romano. Continue to bake for 10 to 15 minutes, or until the cheese is melted and lightly golden brown. Remove the lasagna from the oven and let rest for 15 minutes before serving.

To prepare the arugula pesto: Purée the arugula, basil, garlic, pecorino Romano, olive oil, and pine nuts in a blender until smooth. Season to taste with salt and pepper. If the purée is too thick to spoon around the plate, thin it with a little water or more olive oil. The pesto can be used at room temperature or warmed slightly just prior to use.

ASSEMBLY

Place a 4-inch-square piece of the lasagna in the center of each plate and spoon the arugula pesto and balsamic vinegar around the lasagna. Sprinkle with the basil, pine nuts, and cheese.

WINE NOTES

The layers of cheese and mushrooms in the lasagna could match with red wines, but the addition of the arugula pesto makes reds taste unbalanced and off-key. The perfect note is a lightly oaked, higher-acid, minerally California Chardonnay. The Calcaire Vineyard Chardonnay by Clos du Bois handles the green flavors of the pesto and has a bright acidity that cuts through the weighty richness of the lasagna.

Exotic Mushroom Ragout with Prosciutto and Pattypan Squash

Serves 4

*Rich, sweet prosciutto is just the right foil for the assortment of delectable mushrooms.
Pieces of squash and strands of pickled red onion provide light, clean flavor notes, while basil-infused olive oil
and tiny herbs add the final fresh accents. Wilt a few greens into this mixture and it becomes
a complex warm salad, or place a few strips of chicken breast meat on top for an exciting main course.*

MUSHROOM RAGOUT

1 cup porcini mushrooms
1 cup black trumpet mushrooms
1 cup small morel mushrooms
1 cup hedgehog mushrooms
1 shallot, minced
1½ tablespoons extra virgin olive oil
2 teaspoons balsamic vinegar
¼ cup water
Salt and freshly ground black pepper

SQUASH AND ZUCCHINI

2 teaspoons extra virgin olive oil
8 pattypan squash, quartered
8 baby zucchini, sliced diagonally
¼ cup Pickled Red Onion (see Appendices)
1 tablespoon chopped fresh flat-leaf parsley
Salt and freshly ground black pepper

GARNISH

12 thin slices prosciutto, excess
   fat trimmed
4 teaspoons Basil Oil (see Appendices)
2 tablespoons micro herbs (or chopped
   fresh herbs such as parsley and basil)
Freshly ground black pepper
4 teaspoons extra virgin olive oil

METHOD

To prepare the mushroom ragout: Cut all the mushrooms into bite-size pieces. Place the shallot and olive oil in a sauté pan and cook over medium heat until the shallot is translucent, about 3 minutes. Add the mushrooms and cook for 3 minutes, then add the balsamic vinegar and water. Increase the heat to medium-high and continue to cook the mushrooms until they are tender, about 5 minutes. Season to taste with salt and pepper. Reserve the mushrooms and any juices that remain in the pan separately.

To prepare the squash and zucchini: Heat the olive oil in a sauté pan over medium heat. Add the squash and zucchini and cook for 5 to 7 minutes, or until cooked through. Add the red onion and parsley; season to taste with salt and pepper.

ASSEMBLY

Arrange some of the mushrooms, squash, and zucchini in the center of each plate. Tear the prosciutto into small pieces and interweave with the vegetables. Spoon the reserved mushroom cooking juices around the plate and drizzle with the Basil Oil. Sprinkle the micro herbs around the plate, top with pepper, and drizzle with the olive oil.

WINE NOTES

The earthy flavors of the various wild mushrooms work wonderfully well with light-bodied reds from Italy. Conterno, a classic producer from the Piedmont, crafts a Barbera d'Alba that makes a poignant accompaniment to the pattypans and mushrooms. Or a fruity, well-balanced red from Los Carneros, like Domaine Chandon Pinot Noir, provides a perfect contrast to the saltiness of the prosciutto without overpowering its delicacy.

Hot-and-Sour Shiitake Mushroom Soup with Shrimp Dumplings

Serves 4

Classic hot-and-sour soup is given greater depth here with the addition of shiitake mushrooms.
Luscious shrimp dumplings lend extravagance to what is typically a fairly humble preparation. For an interesting variation,
try substituting veal sweetbreads or shredded duck confit for the shrimp in the dumplings.
Or omit the dumplings altogether and add a piece of poached salmon or cod. The possibilities are almost endless!

SOUP

2 quarts Chicken Stock *(see Appendices)*
1½ cups water
1 pound pork bones with a little
　meat attached
1½ tablespoons cornstarch
3 tablespoons rice wine vinegar
3 tablespoons soy sauce
2 tablespoons Thai fish sauce
¼ teaspoon dried chile flakes
½ pound firm tofu, cut into large dice
6 scallion tops, finely chopped
2 tablespoons toasted sesame oil
10 shiitake mushrooms, julienned

DUMPLINGS

2 teaspoons minced garlic
1 tablespoon minced fresh ginger
2 teaspoons grapeseed oil
10 large shrimp, peeled, deveined, and
　finely chopped
2 tablespoons chopped scallions
2 teaspoons soy sauce
2 teaspoons freshly squeezed yuzu
　citron juice
12 2-inch-square wonton wrappers
1 large egg, lightly beaten

GARNISH

¼ cup micro cilantro leaves
　(or chopped fresh cilantro)

METHOD

To prepare the soup: Place the stock, water, and pork bones in a large saucepan and bring to a boil. Simmer for 5 minutes. Place the cornstarch, vinegar, soy sauce, and fish sauce in a small bowl; whisk together until smooth. Add the cornstarch mixture to the soup and simmer for 5 minutes. Remove the pork bones. Add the chile flakes, tofu, scallions, sesame oil, and mushrooms; simmer for 3 minutes longer.

To prepare the dumplings: Sauté the garlic and ginger in the grapeseed oil over medium heat until fragrant, about 3 minutes. Add the shrimp and cook until the shrimp is almost cooked through, about 5 minutes. Add the scallions, soy sauce, and yuzu citron juice; stir until combined. Remove from the heat and let cool. Lay the wonton wrappers flat on a work surface and lightly brush each edge with the egg. Place 1 heaping teaspoon of the shrimp filling in the center of each wonton; fold the corners of the wontons up toward the center, making square dumplings with a seal that resembles an X. Just before cooking, press the edges firmly together to make sure the seal is tight. Cook the dumplings in boiling salted water for 2 minutes, or until they float to the top. Drain the dumplings and use immediately.

ASSEMBLY

Place 3 dumplings in each bowl and ladle some of the hot soup over them. Sprinkle with the micro cilantro.

WINE NOTES

White and red wines alike tasted off balance against the Japanese flavors in this dish. The soy and brown spices, the shrimp, and the shiitake mushrooms combine to make an extremely flavorful dish, but a difficult one to pair with wine. The best result comes with Kirin Ichiban beer, which highlights the spices and malty flavors of the soup; and the beer's high acidity is palate-cleansing.

Veal and Wild Mushroom Pot Pie

Serves 4

This veal and exotic mushroom pot pie is powerful with its straightforward and earthy flavors.
Once the pot pies are assembled they can be refrigerated until you are ready to bake them,
so from a convenience standpoint they are hard to beat. Best of all, they are practically a meal in themselves;
only a green salad is required as an accompaniment. Turkey, lamb, or pork would all make fine substitutes for the veal.
And feel free to add chiles if you want something with more kick.

FILLING

1 pound veal loin meat, diced
1 tablespoon grapeseed oil
2 tablespoons butter
2 cloves garlic, minced
½ cup small-diced yellow onion
½ cup small-diced carrot
½ cup small-diced parsnip
½ cup small-diced celery
3 cups assorted wild mushrooms
  (such as shiitake, hedgehog, and
  black trumpet), chopped
¼ cup flour
2 cups Chicken Stock *(see Appendices)*
1 tablespoon chopped fresh rosemary
1 tablespoon chopped fresh flat-leaf parsley
1 tablespoon white wine vinegar
¼ cup heavy whipping cream
Salt and freshly ground black pepper

1 tablespoon chopped fresh rosemary
1 tablespoon chopped fresh sage
1 large egg, beaten
4 9-inch puff pastry circles
4 6-inch puff pastry circles

METHOD

To prepare the filling: Brown the veal in the grapeseed oil in a large saucepan over high heat, 7 to 10 minutes. Remove the veal and add the butter, garlic, onion, carrot, parsnip, celery, and mushrooms to the pan. Cook for 10 minutes over medium heat, or until the vegetables are tender. Stir in the flour and cook for 1 minute. Add the stock, herbs, vinegar, and cream; bring the filling to a simmer and cook for 5 minutes. Season to taste with salt and pepper. Let cool before using and drain any excess liquid from the filling.

To prepare the pot pies: Preheat the oven to 400°F. Combine the rosemary, sage, and egg in a small bowl. Place four 5-inch-diameter by 2-inch-high pie tins on a sheet pan; line the bottom of each tin with a 9-inch puff pastry circle. Fill the tins to the top with the pot pie filling and cover each with a 6-inch puff pastry circle. Firmly crimp the pastry edges together and brush with the egg mixture. Bake the pot pies for 20 to 25 minutes, or until golden brown. Serve immediately.

WINE NOTES

This pot pie can be matched with both a red and a white—an achievement that will astound your guests! A fuller-bodied red Burgundy, such as Domaine Leroy or Domaine Fourrier, stands up to the rich veal and mushroom combination. On the other hand, Bernard Morey's Chassagne-Montrachet is a white Burgundy that complements the toasty, buttery crust and has the acidity to lighten the dish. It will be difficult to choose your favorite.

Crispy Bass with Trumpet Royal Mushroom–Oxtail Crust and Red Wine–Mushroom Sauce

Serves 4

This preparation nicely demonstrates how mushrooms, even when used merely as an accent (here mixed with braised oxtail to form a crust for sea bass), can profoundly affect the overall tone of a dish. Sea bass or virtually any fish, for that matter — gains so much complexity from the mushroom component that scarcely anything else is needed. A little bit of braised chard and a red wine mushroom sauce made with the oxtail pan juices finish off a stunning combination. Served in small portions, this dish would be a wonderful starter for a roasted meat entrée.

BRAISED OXTAILS

4 oxtails (about 1 pound)
2 tablespoons canola oil
1 yellow onion, chopped
1 carrot, chopped
1 stalk celery, chopped
2 cloves garlic, chopped
1 tomato, seeded and coarsely chopped
1 cup red wine
2 cups Chicken Stock (*see Appendices*)
1 bay leaf
2 sprigs thyme
Salt and freshly ground black pepper

RED WINE–MUSHROOM SAUCE

¼ cup small-diced bacon
3 cups trumpet royal mushrooms, quartered
2 shallots, peeled and thinly sliced
1 clove garlic, minced
2 tablespoons extra virgin olive oil
1 cup red wine
½ cup braising liquid from the oxtails (above)
Salt and freshly ground black pepper

BASS

2 teaspoons grapeseed oil
4 2½-ounce pieces bass fillet, skin on
Salt and freshly ground black pepper

SWISS CHARD

1 tablespoon butter
1 tablespoon minced shallot
2 cups chopped stemmed Swiss chard
Salt and freshly ground black pepper

GARNISH

¼ cup micro cilantro (or chopped fresh cilantro)
4 teaspoons Herb Oil (*see Appendices*)

METHOD

To prepare the oxtails: Preheat the oven to 325°F. Cook the oxtails with the canola oil in a small roasting pan on the stove top over medium-high heat for 3 minutes on each side, or until golden brown. Remove the oxtails and set aside. Add the onion, carrot, celery, garlic, and tomato to the pan; cook for 7 to 10 minutes, or until golden brown and caramelized. Return the oxtails to the pan and add the wine, stock, bay leaf, and thyme. Season with salt and pepper. Cover the pan tightly and roast in the oven for 3 hours, or until the meat is very tender. Remove the meat from the bones and discard the bones. Season the meat to taste with salt and pepper. Strain the braising liquid through a fine-mesh sieve and skim off any excess fat. Reserve ½ cup of the strained braising liquid for the sauce.

To prepare the sauce: Render the fat from the bacon in a sauté pan over medium heat, about 4 minutes. Add the mushrooms, shallots, garlic, and olive oil; continue to cook for 5 minutes. Add the wine and cook for 10 minutes, or until the wine is reduced by half. Add the reserved ½ cup braising liquid and season to taste with salt and pepper. Remove one-third of the mushrooms and finely chop them. Fold the finely chopped mushrooms into the braised oxtail meat.

To prepare the bass: Heat the grapeseed oil in a sauté pan over medium-high heat. Season the bass with salt and pepper. Add the bass to the pan skin side down and cook for 4 minutes, or until the skin is golden brown and crispy. Flip the fish over and continue to cook for 1 to 2 minutes, or until just cooked through. Remove the fish from the pan and carefully remove the crispy skin by cutting it off in one piece with a knife. Reserve both the skin and the fish.

To prepare the Swiss chard: Place the butter and shallot in a sauté pan and cook over medium heat until the shallot is translucent, about 3 minutes. Add the chard and cook for 3 to 5 minutes, or until the chard is just wilted. Season to taste with salt and pepper.

ASSEMBLY

Place some of the chard in the center of each plate. Place a piece of the bass atop the chard; crust it with a generous amount of the oxtail mixture, and top with a piece of the crispy skin. Spoon some of the sauce around the plate. Sprinkle with the micro cilantro and drizzle the Herb Oil around the plate.

WINE NOTES

Sautéed bass alone could harmonize with either white or red wine, but the red wine-mushroom sauce and the oxtail crust produce a finer pairing with earthy reds. In the Burgundy region of France, Hubert Lignier produces Pinot Noir with impeccable balance and elegance. His Morey-Saint-Denis heightens the earthy elements of the dish while not overshadowing the flavor of the bass; the wine works particularly well with the meatiness of the trumpet royal mushrooms.

Lobster-Stuffed Shiitake Mushrooms with Chive Crème Fraîche

Serves 4

Elegant and attractive, these stuffed mushrooms make great canapés or hors d'oeuvres for a special dinner. Two or three of them could be served on a plate with a splash of shallot vinaigrette as an engaging first course. Scallops or shrimp could certainly stand in for the lobster; or take the recipe in a completely different direction with shredded braised pork.

STUFFED MUSHROOMS

1 clove garlic, minced
1 tablespoon minced shallot
2 tablespoons butter
¾ pound lobster meat, cooked and
    cut into small dice
½ cup small-diced Granny Smith apple
½ cup panko (Japanese breadcrumbs)
1 tablespoon chopped fresh chives
1 tablespoon chopped fresh flat-leaf parsley
½ cup grated Monterey Jack cheese
Salt and freshly ground black pepper
12 large shiitake mushrooms, stemmed

CHIVE CRÈME FRAÎCHE

¾ cup crème fraîche
2 tablespoons heavy whipping cream
2 tablespoons chopped fresh chives
1 tablespoon freshly squeezed lemon juice
1 tablespoon water
Salt and freshly ground black pepper

METHOD

To prepare the mushrooms: Preheat the oven to 350°F. Sauté the garlic and shallot in the butter over medium heat until translucent, about 3 minutes. Remove from the heat and add the lobster meat, apple, breadcrumbs, chives, parsley, and cheese. Toss to combine and season to taste with salt and pepper. Line a sheet pan with parchment paper. Place the mushroom caps on the prepared sheet pan. Fill the mushrooms generously with the lobster filling and bake for 10 to 12 minutes, or until the cheese is melted.

To prepare the chive crème fraîche: Combine the crème fraîche, cream, chives, lemon juice, and water in a bowl. Season to taste with salt and pepper.

ASSEMBLY

Spoon a wide line of the crème fraîche mixture down the center of each plate. Set 3 stuffed mushrooms in a line over the mixture and top with freshly ground black pepper.

WINE NOTES

The lobster and crème fraîche in this dish cause oaky wines to taste disjointed and bitter. Unoaked versions of Italian whites, such as Gavi or Soave, work exceptionally well to bring out the Granny Smith apple and heighten the mineral flavor of the lobster. The high acidity from Michele Chiarlo's Gavi is also able to trim the richness of the Monterey Jack cheese.

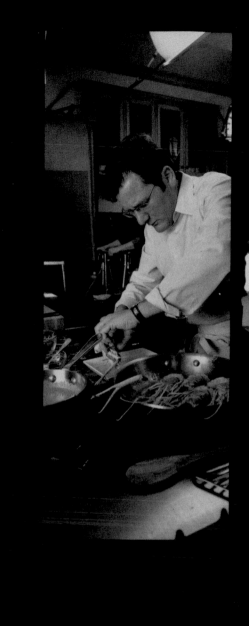

ONIONS

Langoustines with Green Curry Sauce and Roasted Pearl Onions and Scallions

Serves 4

Langoustines (or, if you choose, lobster or shrimp) and scallions come off as superstars when paired with this green curry sauce. The aromas and flavors meld into something both exotic and ethereal. Small pearl onions, while slightly sweet, provide just the right bite to cut into the shellfish and the intoxicating curry sauce. Baby lettuces are just wilted, and golden beets nicely round out this glorious combination of tastes.

VEGETABLES

8 baby golden beets, unpeeled
12 purple pearl onions, unpeeled
3 sprigs thyme
2 tablespoons extra virgin olive oil
12 scallions, trimmed
Salt and freshly ground black pepper

GREEN CURRY SAUCE

6 scallions, chopped
6 jalapeño chiles, seeded and chopped
2 cloves garlic, chopped
1 tablespoon minced fresh ginger
1 tablespoon coriander seeds, toasted
  and crushed
½ teaspoon freshly ground black pepper
4 fresh kaffir lime leaves, torn
2 stalks lemongrass, chopped
2 cups loosely packed chopped fresh
  basil leaves
1 bunch cilantro with stems, chopped
3 tablespoons extra virgin olive oil
4 limes, zested and juiced
¼ cup unsweetened coconut milk
Salt

LANGOUSTINES

2 shallots, minced
2 tablespoons Shellfish Oil
  (see Appendices)
8 langoustines, shells removed
Salt and freshly ground black pepper
2 cups firmly packed baby lettuce leaves

GARNISH

4 teaspoons Shellfish Oil *(see Appendices)*
4 teaspoons chiffonade-cut fresh basil
Freshly ground black pepper

METHOD

To prepare the vegetables: Preheat the oven to 350°F. Place the beets, onions, thyme, and olive oil in an ovenproof pan. Cover the vegetables and roast for 30 minutes. Add the scallions and replace the cover. Continue to roast for 20 more minutes, or until the vegetables are tender. Peel the onions and beets and cut the beets in half. Season to taste with salt and pepper.

To prepare the sauce: In a blender, purée the scallions, chiles, garlic, ginger, coriander, black pepper, lime leaves, lemongrass, basil, cilantro, olive oil, and lime zest and juice; pass through a fine-mesh sieve. Add the coconut milk and season to taste with salt and pepper. Warm just prior to use.

To prepare the langoustines: Heat a sauté pan over medium heat. Add the shallots and Shellfish Oil and cook for 2 minutes. Add the langoustines. Increase the heat to high and continue to cook the langoustines for 2 to 3 minutes on each side, or until just cooked through. Remove the langoustines from the pan and season to taste with salt and pepper. Add the lettuce to the same pan and quickly wilt it in the hot pan; transfer to a bowl and season to taste with salt and pepper. Slice each langoustine into 4 pieces.

ASSEMBLY

Cover the center of each plate with a generous amount of the green curry sauce. Arrange some of the wilted lettuce, langoustines, and vegetables on top of the sauce. Drizzle the Shellfish Oil around the plate and top with the basil chiffonade and pepper.

WINE NOTES

This dish is a sommelier's dream! Nearly every white wine is successful with it; the only differences are the ingredients highlighted. A Meursault from Arnaud Ente accentuates the citrus qualities of the sauce without masking the tantalizing flavor of the langoustines. The mineral flavors are emphasized by Domaine Louis Michel's unoaked version of Chablis. Riesling Kabinett from Zilliken in the Mosel-Saar-Ruwer has a hint of sweetness that contrasts well with the spiciness in the curry sauce.

Cod with Red Onion–Rhubarb Marmalade and Cipolline Onions

Serves 4

The onion components of this dish make their presence known, yet they are subtle enough to allow the fish to be the star. The marmalade has a sweet-and-sour flavor that cuts nicely into the delicate richness of the fish. Fragrant cipolline onions are puréed to a silky smoothness, with Thai chiles adding just the right amount of kick to liven up this perfect exclamation point for the dish. Ultimately, although the various elements are straightforward, the total combination is quite sophisticated.

ONIONS AND ONION PURÉE

16 cipolline onions, peeled
1½ cups Chicken Stock *(see Appendices)*
2 dried Thai chiles
1 tablespoon butter
2 tablespoons sherry wine vinegar
10 leaves fresh basil
1 clove garlic
Salt and freshly ground black pepper

MARMALADE

2 cups small-diced rhubarb
1 cup small-diced red onion
½ cup red wine vinegar
¼ cup maple sugar
3 sprigs thyme
1 clove garlic, minced
Salt and freshly ground black pepper

COD

2 teaspoons grapeseed oil
4 4-ounce cod fillets
Salt and freshly ground black pepper

GARNISH

4 teaspoons chiffonade-cut fresh basil
Freshly ground black pepper

METHOD

To prepare the onions and purée: Preheat the oven to 350°F. Combine the onions, stock, chiles, butter, vinegar, basil, and garlic in an ovenproof pan. Cover and cook for 45 minutes, or until the onions are tender. Purée 8 of the onions in a blender with just enough of the braising liquid to purée smoothly. Season the purée to taste with salt and pepper. Reheat in a small saucepan just prior to use, if necessary. Cut the remaining onions in half and season to taste with salt and pepper.

To prepare the marmalade: Combine the rhubarb, onion, vinegar, sugar, thyme, and garlic in a saucepan. Cook over medium-low heat for 30 minutes, or until the rhubarb has dissolved. Season to taste with salt and pepper.

To prepare the cod: Heat the grapeseed oil in a sauté pan over medium-high heat. Season the cod with salt and pepper and add to the pan. Cook for 3 minutes on each side, or until just cooked through.

ASSEMBLY

In the center of each plate, place 4 onion halves. Crust the cod with the marmalade and place on top of the onions. Spoon the onion purée around the cod and sprinkle with the basil. Top with pepper.

WINE NOTES

Rosé Champagne is generally overlooked when it comes to food and wine matchups, but its cleansing acidity and fruity aromas can create magical pairings. The red onion and rhubarb marmalade is perfect with Godmé's rosé from the Verzenay village in Champagne. The rosé doesn't mask the restrained flavor of the cod, while the intense marmalade actually brings out the wine's fruitiness.

Leek Confit Soup with Olive Oil–Poached Salmon and Basmati Rice Cake

Serves 4

Leek soup is a crowd favorite, and this preparation presents it at its hearty best. A piece of meltingly soft, satiny-rich olive oil–poached salmon is gloriously elegant. By way of contrast, the basmati rice cake provides a nutty taste and a bit of substance. Overall, the flavors combine into something that is almost sinfully luxurious. I suppose if one really wanted to gild the lily, black truffles could be shaved all over the top. For an intriguing variation, try substituting pieces of chicken breast tempura for the salmon.

SOUP

3 leeks (white part only), cleaned
2 cups extra virgin olive oil
2 sprigs rosemary
2 sprigs thyme
2 bay leaves
2½ cups Chicken Stock *(see Appendices)*
1 teaspoon apple cider vinegar
Salt and freshly ground black pepper

RICE CAKES

2 cloves garlic, minced
2 shallots, minced
1 tablespoon extra virgin olive oil
½ cup basmati rice
1¼ cups Chicken Stock *(see Appendices)*
Salt and freshly ground black pepper
¼ cup pine nuts, toasted and
    coarsely chopped
1 tablespoon grapeseed oil

SALMON

4 4-ounce salmon fillets, skin off
½ bunch flat-leaf parsley
2 sprigs rosemary
4 cups extra virgin olive oil
Salt and freshly ground black pepper

LEEK

1 leek (white part only), cleaned
1 tablespoon chopped fresh flat-leaf parsley
2 teaspoons extra virgin olive oil
1 teaspoon freshly squeezed lime juice
Salt and freshly ground black pepper

GARNISH

4 teaspoons micro opal basil (or chopped
    opal basil)
Freshly ground black pepper

METHOD

To prepare the soup: Preheat the oven to 250°F. Place the leeks, olive oil, and herbs in an ovenproof pan and cook, covered, for 4 hours, or until the leeks are very tender. Remove the leeks and chop coarsely. Place the leeks in a blender and purée with the stock and vinegar until smooth. Pass through a fine-mesh sieve if stringy and season to taste with salt and pepper. Place in a saucepan and reheat just prior to use.

To prepare the rice cakes: In a medium saucepan, sauté the garlic and shallots in the olive oil over medium heat until translucent, about 5 minutes. Add the rice and stir to coat with the oil. Add the stock, cover, and simmer for 20 minutes, or until the rice is cooked. Season the rice with salt and pepper and fold in the pine nuts. Line a 6-inch-square pan with parchment paper. Spread the rice out in the prepared pan; cover with a second sheet of parchment and press a second pan of the same size over the rice to pack it down. Refrigerate for 2 hours.

Cut the rice cake into four 3-inch squares. Just prior to serving, sauté the rice cakes in the grapeseed oil in a nonstick pan over high heat until golden brown and crispy.

To prepare the salmon: Place the salmon, herbs, and olive oil in a small straight-sided sauté pan with 3-inch-high sides (make sure the salmon is covered by the olive oil). Place the pan over a burner and heat the oil to 130°F. Continue to cook at that temperature, but no hotter. Poach the salmon for 20 minutes. The salmon will remain bright pink-orange, but when touched it will feel tender and break apart under slight pressure. Remove the salmon from the oil and season to taste with salt and pepper.

To prepare the leek: Julienne the leek and blanch in boiling salted water. Drain and toss with the parsley, olive oil, and lime juice. Season to taste with salt and pepper.

ASSEMBLY

Place 1 crispy rice cake in the center of each shallow serving bowl. Place a piece of the salmon on top of the rice cake and arrange some of the julienned leeks over the salmon. Ladle some of the soup around the rice cake. Sprinkle with the opal basil and top with pepper.

WINE NOTES

Salmon poached in olive oil melts in your mouth like butter on a warm roll. High-acid whites like Riesling or Sauvignon Blanc would be jarring with this unctuous texture. Robert Sinskey Pinot Blanc from Los Carneros has a rounder style, with a wealth of brown spices that are echoed in the basmati rice cake. This wine is a subtle and more harmonious pairing than especially aromatic wines.

Duck Breast with Braised Vidalia Onions and Cannellini Beans

Serves 4

This entrée, while exhibiting a sensual earthiness, is actually quite refined in its flavors and textures.
The marriage of onions, cannellini beans, and watercress provides the perfect
subtle backdrop for the duck. Fragrant notes of cinnamon and juniper add a playful accent.
Chicken, pork tenderloin, or salmon would be admirable substitutions here.

BEANS

¼ cup large-diced bacon
1 stalk celery, cut into 3 large pieces
1 carrot, peeled and cut into 3 large pieces
1 small yellow onion, cut into large pieces
1 cup cannellini beans, soaked overnight
    in water
4 cloves garlic
2 tablespoons butter
Salt and freshly ground black pepper

ONIONS AND ONION-BEAN PURÉE

3 small Vidalia onions, peeled with root
    end left attached
12 purple pearl onions, peeled
1 cinnamon stick
3 whole cloves
1 red Thai chile
4 juniper berries, toasted and crushed
2 bay leaves
1 clove garlic
2 cups Chicken Stock *(see Appendices)*
1 cup cooked beans (above)
Salt and freshly ground black pepper

DUCK

2 duck breasts, skin scored
Salt and freshly ground black pepper
1½ cups loosely packed watercress,
    thick stems discarded
1 tablespoon minced shallot

GARNISH

½ cup hot Meat Stock Reduction
    (see Appendices)
4 teaspoons Basil Oil *(see Appendices)*
¼ cup micro herbs (or chopped fresh herbs)
Freshly ground black pepper

METHOD

To prepare the beans: Render the bacon in a saucepan over low heat until all the fat is released, about 5 minutes. Add the vegetables and cook until lightly caramelized, about 5 minutes. Drain the beans and add to the vegetables with the garlic and butter; pour in water to cover. Simmer over low heat, stirring occasionally, for 2 hours, or until the beans are very tender. Discard the vegetables and bacon pieces and season the beans to taste with salt and pepper. Reserve 1 cup of the beans separately.

To prepare the onions and purée: Preheat the oven to 325˚F. Cut the Vidalia onions into sixths, keeping the root end attached (this will help keep the pieces from falling apart during cooking). Place all the onions, the spices and herbs, the garlic, and the stock in an ovenproof pan with a lid. Cook, covered, for 1 hour, or until the onions are tender. Transfer 6 pieces of the Vidalia onion and any cooking liquid that remains in the pan to a blender; add the 1 cup reserved beans. Purée until smooth and season to taste with salt and pepper. Reheat the purée and roasted onions just prior to use, if necessary.

To prepare the duck: Season the duck breasts with salt and pepper and place in a very hot sauté pan, skin side down. Cook for 3 to 4 minutes on each side, or until the skin is golden brown and crispy and the duck is medium-rare. Allow the duck to rest for 2 minutes, then thinly slice on the diagonal. Drain the fat from the pan. Place the watercress and shallot in the same pan; quickly wilt and season to taste with salt and pepper.

ASSEMBLY

Spoon some of the onion-bean purée in an oval ring on each plate. Arrange some of the onion pieces and whole beans on the right side of the oval, allowing a few pieces to cascade toward the other side. Arrange some of the duck slices and wilted watercress, overlapping, on the right side of the plate. Spoon the warmed stock reduction around the plate. Drizzle the Basil Oil around the plate and sprinkle with the micro herbs. Top with pepper.

WINE NOTES

There is a stunning complexity of flavor in this dish. The earthy aspects of the roasted duck and the spiced braised onions require a medium- to full-bodied Italian red from Tuscany. Gagliole *rosso* has the structure to stand up to the duck, along with spice elements that pair well with the braised onions. As a counterbalance to the fattiness of the duck, this Tuscan red has a cleansing acidity.

Roasted Garlic and Morel Mushroom Ravioli with Red Wine–Olive Sauce

Serves 4

*Few flavors are headier than that of roasted garlic, with its profound and intriguing aroma.
Here it is used, along with morel mushrooms, Kalamata olives, and Parmesan cheese, as a filling for ravioli.
The result is a clean but complex medley of flavors. The ravioli are paired with a simple ragout
of spring vegetables that provides extraordinary flavor and texture notes. A robust red wine–olive sauce weaves
all the components together, while a delicate basil sauce helps keep things vibrant and sprightly.
Slices of pork or lamb loin could be added to compose a hearty main course.*

RAVIOLI

2 cups extra-fine semolina flour
3 eggs, lightly beaten
1 shallot, minced
1 tablespoon extra virgin olive oil
2 cups morel mushrooms, chopped
⅓ cup chopped Kalamata olives
16 cloves Roasted Garlic *(see Appendices)*
3 scallions, chopped
2 tablespoons grated Parmesan cheese
Salt and freshly ground black pepper
1 egg, lightly beaten, for sealing ravioli

RAGOUT

1 small Vidalia onion, julienned
2 tablespoons butter
1½ cups morel mushrooms
2 tablespoons water
8 pencil-thin stalks asparagus, blanched
  and cut diagonally into 2-inch pieces
1 cup shucked fava beans, blanched
  and peeled
8 ramps, cleaned and blanched
1 teaspoon balsamic vinegar
Salt and freshly ground black pepper

RED WINE–OLIVE SAUCE

½ cup Meat Stock Reduction
  (see Appendices)
½ cup Red Wine Reduction
  (see Appendices)
½ cup sliced Kalamata olives

BASIL SAUCE

½ cup loosely packed chopped fresh
  basil leaves
⅓ cup extra virgin olive oil
1 tablespoon pine nuts
1 tablespoon grated Parmesan cheese
1 teaspoon balsamic vinegar
Salt and freshly ground black pepper

GARNISH

4 teaspoons chopped opal basil
Freshly ground black pepper

METHOD

To prepare the ravioli: Place the semolina flour and the 3 beaten eggs in the bowl of an electric mixer fitted with the paddle attachment; mix on low speed for 3 minutes, or until the dough comes together. Form the dough into a ball and cover with plastic wrap. Refrigerate for at least 1 hour before using.

Sauté the shallot in the olive oil over medium heat for 2 minutes, or until translucent. Add the mushrooms and cook for 2 more minutes. Add the olives, garlic, and scallions; cook for 2 minutes, or until all the flavors blend. Remove from the heat and cool to room temperature. Add the cheese and season to taste with salt and pepper. Refrigerate until ready to use.

Using a pasta machine, roll out the semolina pasta into ¹⁄₁₆-inch-thick sheets. (The number of sheets produced will vary depending on the width of the machine.) Cut the pasta sheets into a total of twelve 2¾-inch circles and twelve 3-inch circles. Place 1 tablespoon of the filling in the center of each 2¾-inch pasta circle. Lightly brush the edges of the pasta with the remaining 1 egg; cover with a 3-inch pasta circle and gently press the edges together to seal. Repeat until you have assembled 12 ravioli. Cook the ravioli in boiling salted water for 3 to 4 minutes, or until al dente.

To prepare the ragout: Sauté the onion in the butter in a sauté pan over medium heat until the onion begins to caramelize, 7 to 10 minutes. Add the mushrooms and water; continue to cook for 3 minutes, or until the mushrooms are tender. Add the asparagus, beans, ramps, and vinegar; cook until all the ingredients are hot. Season to taste with salt and pepper.

To prepare the wine sauce: Warm all the ingredients together in a small saucepan over medium heat.

To prepare the basil sauce: Combine the basil, olive oil, pine nuts, cheese, and vinegar in a mortar; grind with the pestle to form a coarse paste. Season to taste with salt and pepper.

ASSEMBLY

Arrange 3 ravioli in the center of each plate. Spoon the ragout over the ravioli and sprinkle with the chopped opal basil. Spoon the wine and basil sauces over the ravioli and around the plate. Top with pepper.

WINE NOTES

Supertuscans—usually blends of Sangiovese, Cabernet Sauvignon, and Cabernet Franc—are tremendous food wines. The high acidity of Convivio, which is a 75 percent Sangiovese and 25 percent Cabernet Sauvignon *vino da tavola* from Tuscany, is in harmony with the intense olive and red wine sauce and the hearty ravioli. All the powerful components of this dish actually cause the Convivio to taste more fruit-forward.

Chilled Spring Pea Soup with Mussel, Elephant Garlic, and Fiddlehead Fern–Stuffed Red Onions

Serves 4

The light but explosive flavors in this dish are a celebration of springtime.
Each half of a magnificent red onion contains such a medley of delectable morsels,
this soup could serve as a meal unto itself. Lobster or shrimp can easily stand in for the mussels.
To suit the occasion, you can convert the soup to a warm or hot preparation.

SOUP

1 pound sugar snap peas, blanched
½ cup extra virgin olive oil
2 cups water
1 clove Roasted Elephant Garlic
 (see Appendices)
Salt and freshly ground black pepper

STUFFED ONIONS

2 red onions, peeled and halved horizontally
1 tablespoon extra virgin olive oil
1 tablespoon butter
1 teaspoon minced garlic
1 cup firmly packed fiddlehead ferns
1 cup sugar snap peas, blanched and
 thinly sliced diagonally
20 mussels, cooked (unopened mussels
 discarded) and shelled, juices reserved
4 cloves Roasted Elephant Garlic
 (see Appendices), quartered
2 tablespoons Tarragon Oil
 (see Appendices)
2 teaspoons chopped fresh tarragon
Salt and freshly ground black pepper

GARNISH

¼ cup crème fraîche
1 tablespoon water
Salt and freshly ground black pepper
1 tablespoon Tarragon Oil
 (see Appendices)
1 teaspoon chopped fresh tarragon

METHOD

To prepare the soup: Place the sugar snap peas, olive oil, water, and garlic in a blender; purée until smooth. Pass the soup through a fine-mesh sieve if fibrous, then season to taste with salt and pepper. Refrigerate the soup until ready to serve.

To prepare the stuffed onions: Preheat the oven to 325°F. Rub the onions, especially the cut side, with the olive oil and place cut side down in an ovenproof pan. Cover the onions and roast for 1 hour, or until the onions are tender. Remove the onions from the pan and carefully remove the inner rings (if the outermost ring is dried out from the roasting, discard that ring first), leaving the two outer rings intact.

Place the butter, garlic, and fiddlehead ferns in a sauté pan over medium heat and cook for 3 to 5 minutes, or until the ferns are tender. Add the sugar snap peas, mussels, reserved mussel juice, garlic, Tarragon Oil, and tarragon. Toss the filling and season to taste with salt and pepper. Remove from the heat. Fill each hollowed-out onion half with some of the filling.

ASSEMBLY

In a small bowl, whisk together the crème fraîche and water; season to taste with salt and pepper. Place a stuffed onion in the center of each shallow serving bowl. Ladle the chilled soup into the bowls and spoon some of the crème fraîche mixture around the stuffed onion. Combine the Tarragon Oil and tarragon and drizzle the mixture around the soup.

WINE NOTES

The green flavor of the fiddleheads and spring peas pushes the wine pairing toward Sauvignon Blanc, but the addition of crème fraîche rounds out the dish and causes examples from the Old World to taste excessively tart. Moraga, from Bel Air, California, makes a rounder-style Sauvignon Blanc that suits the soup. Prager's Grüner Veltliner from the Wachau in Austria has a hint of residual sugar that balances with the sweetness of the roasted onions.

POTATOES

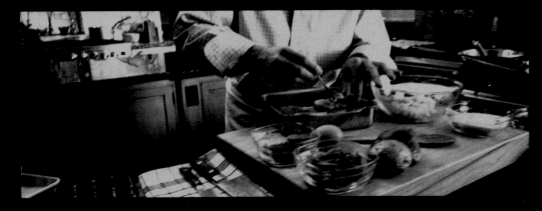

Duck Confit–Stuffed Twice-Baked Fingerling Potato

Serves 4

This recipe can serve as a satisfying small appetizer (by offering just a single potato) or as something more substantial. The great thing is that all the work on the potatoes can be done in advance, and then they can simply be popped into the oven at the last moment. Try substituting lobster meat for the duck confit as a variation.

TWICE-BAKED POTATOES

4 large fingerling potatoes
1 large Yukon Gold potato
2 large egg yolks
3 tablespoons chopped fresh chives
¼ cup shredded Duck Confit,
   (see Appendices)
Salt and freshly ground black pepper

BROCCOFLOWER

1½ cups broccoflower, cut into
   1-inch florets
2 tablespoons butter
Salt and freshly ground black pepper

SAUCE

½ cup Meat Stock Reduction
   (see Appendices)
¼ cup shredded Duck Confit,
   (see Appendices)

DUCK CONFIT

4 2-ounce pieces Duck Confit *(see Appendices)*, skin on, bones removed

GARNISH

2 tablespoons micro herbs (or chopped
   fresh herbs)
Freshly ground black pepper

METHOD

To prepare the potatoes: Preheat the oven to 350°F. Bake the fingerling and Yukon Gold potatoes until done; the fingerlings take about 40 minutes, and the Yukon Gold about 15 minutes longer. Scrape all the flesh out of the Yukon Gold potato and discard the skin. Cut off just the top quarter of the fingerlings and hollow out the potatoes, keeping the shape intact. Add the flesh from the fingerlings to the Yukon Gold flesh and pass through a ricer. Place the riced potatoes in a mixing bowl and fold in the egg yolks, chives, and shredded confit. Season to taste with salt and pepper. Fill the reserved fingerling potato skins generously with the filling. A half hour before serving, preheat the oven to 375°F. Place the potatoes in an ovenproof pan and bake for 20 minutes.

To prepare the broccoflower: Sauté the broccoflower with the butter over medium-high heat for 7 to 10 minutes, or until caramelized. Season to taste with salt and pepper.

To prepare the sauce: Combine the stock reduction and shredded confit in a small saucepan and warm over medium heat until hot.

To prepare the duck confit: Just prior to serving, heat a sauté pan over medium-high heat. Place the confit skin side down and cook for 4 minutes, or until the skin is golden brown and crispy. Flip over and continue to cook for 2 minutes, or until just hot.

ASSEMBLY

On each plate, place a twice-baked potato at 10 o'clock. Place a small amount of the broccoflower at 2 o'clock and a piece of the crispy duck confit at 6 o'clock. Spoon some of the heated sauce around the plate and sprinkle with the micro herbs. Top with pepper.

WINE NOTES

Domaine Dujac produces some of the most elegant, feminine, and balanced wines in all of Burgundy. The pretty raspberry and cherry notes are set off by undertones of wet earth and surrounded by the aroma of violets and roses. All these complex elements have a firm acid backbone, which cuts through the velvety twice-baked potatoes. The duck confit contrasts well with the fruitiness of the wine. Clos Saint-Denis and Echézeaux are two of the best *grands crus* from this domaine.

Potato Soup with Poached Oysters and Crispy Potatoes

Serves 4

*Simple to prepare, this soup demonstrates why potatoes are so universally loved.
Crispy potato strands add a fantastic textural note and augment the potato taste. Oysters, which have been
just warmed through, provide a luxurious sensuality, and bacon lardons add smoky meatiness.
A sprinkling of herbs and a drizzle of Herb Oil are all that is needed to round out the flavors.
If you serve whole roast chicken with black truffles as the entrée, you will have the perfect meal.*

SOUP

6 small Yukon Gold potatoes,
  peeled and diced
1 quart water
1 bay leaf
Salt
½ cup crème fraîche
½ lemon, juiced
Freshly ground black pepper

SOUP GARNISH

1 cup bacon lardons
1 leek, cleaned and cut into ¼-inch rings
1 clove garlic, minced
1 tablespoon chopped fresh parsley
Freshly ground black pepper

OYSTERS

24 small oysters, shucked, juices
  reserved and strained
3 tablespoons freshly squeezed
  lemon juice
1 tablespoon chopped fresh parsley
1 tablespoon lemon zest
2 tablespoons minced shallot
½ cup extra virgin olive oil
Salt and freshly ground black pepper

POTATOES

1 small russet potato, peeled and finely
  julienned
2 tablespoons flour
Salt and freshly ground black pepper
1 cup grapeseed oil

GARNISH

2 tablespoons Herb Oil *(see Appendices)*
2 tablespoons micro herbs (or chopped
  fresh herbs)

METHOD

To prepare the soup: Place the potatoes, water, and bay leaf in a large saucepan and season with salt. Bring to a simmer and cook until the potatoes are tender, about 10 minutes. Remove the bay leaf and purée the potatoes and water in a food processor until smooth. Whisk in the crème fraîche and lemon juice. Just prior to serving, season to taste with salt and pepper and warm over medium heat.

To prepare the soup garnish: Render the bacon in a sauté pan over medium heat, about 5 minutes. Add the leeks and garlic. Continue to cook until the leeks are tender and the bacon is crispy, about 5 minutes. Add the parsley and season with pepper.

To prepare the oysters: Place the reserved oyster juice in a saucepan and add the oysters. Warm over medium heat until the oysters are just warm and beginning to become firm. Remove the oysters from the liquid. Whisk the lemon juice, parsley, zest, shallot, and olive oil into the oyster juice; season to taste with salt and pepper. Return the oysters to the saucepan and reheat just prior to use, if necessary.

To prepare the potatoes: Lightly dredge the julienned potato in the flour and season with salt and pepper. Form the julienned potato into small disks 2 inches in diameter. Heat the grapeseed oil in a sauté pan until hot. Fry the potatoes in the oil for 3 to 4 minutes on each side, or until golden brown and crispy. Transfer the potato disks to paper towels and blot. Season with salt. Select the best 4 disks and set aside (reserve any remaining disks for snacking).

ASSEMBLY

Place some of the soup garnish in the bottom of each shallow serving bowl and carefully balance a crispy potato disk over it. Arrange 2 of the oysters on top of the potato and 4 more in the bowl. Ladle the soup around the oysters, being careful not to cover the crispy potato. Drizzle the Herb Oil into the soup and sprinkle with the micro herbs.

WINE NOTES

In the past it has been difficult to use the words "value" and "Champagne" in the same sentence, but this no longer holds true. The wines of small grower-producers are exciting and can be purchased at a fraction of the cost of bottles from large Champagne houses. Guy Larmandier's *grand cru* Blanc de Blancs is an excellent example that elevates the mineral flavors of the oysters and the lemon in the soup. This bright, clean, 100 percent Chardonnay Champagne also contrasts well with the bacon and the leeks.

Three-Potato Salad with White Truffle Mayonnaise and Preserved Celery and Radishes

Serves 4

This is a classic potato salad with an elegant twist. The white truffle mayonnaise has an ethereal flavor that elevates the humble tuber. Pieces of preserved celery and radish provide not only an acidic accent, but also a textural counterpoint to the mild, almost creamy potatoes. This dish is a fantastic accompaniment for a piece of grilled fish or chicken, or a small amount of it can be placed on a bed of greens to make a remarkable salad.

PRESERVED CELERY AND RADISHES

1 cup Pickling Brine *(see Appendices)*
1 celery stalk, peeled and thinly
   sliced diagonally
8 red radishes, cut into eighths

WHITE TRUFFLE MAYONNAISE

1 tablespoon freshly squeezed lemon juice
1 large egg yolk
½ cup white truffle oil
Salt and freshly ground white pepper

POTATO SALAD

6 medium banana fingerling potatoes,
   boiled and cut into small wedges
2 small Yukon Gold potatoes, boiled
   and cut into small wedges
6 small Red Bliss potatoes, boiled and
   cut into sixths
2 teaspoons chopped fresh chives
2 teaspoons chopped fresh tarragon
2 teaspoons chopped fresh flat-leaf parsley
2 teaspoons chopped fresh thyme
2 scallions (white parts only), thinly
   sliced diagonally
¼ cup white truffle mayonnaise (above)
Salt and freshly ground black pepper

GARNISH

2 tablespoons white truffle oil
1 tablespoon chopped celery leaves
Freshly ground black pepper

METHOD

To prepare the celery and radishes: Warm the brine in a small saucepan; add the celery and radish pieces. Remove from the heat and allow the vegetables to steep at room temperature for 2 hours. Drain the vegetables.

To prepare the mayonnaise: Place the lemon juice and egg yolk in a small bowl. Slowly whisk in the white truffle oil until all the oil is incorporated and the mixture has a mayonnaise-like consistency. Season to taste with salt and white pepper.

To prepare the potato salad: Cool all the potato wedges to room temperature. Place the potatoes in a mixing bowl and toss together with the chopped herbs and scallions. Add the mayonnaise and toss until incorporated. Season to taste with salt and pepper.

ASSEMBLY

Spoon an oval ring of the white truffle mayonnaise on each plate. Arrange the potato salad inside the mayonnaise ring. Sprinkle the celery and radishes around the potatoes. Drizzle the white truffle oil over the potatoes and around the plate. Sprinkle the celery leaves over the potatoes. Top with pepper.

WINE NOTES

Potato and white truffle is a classic combination in northwestern Italy. The acidity of the preserved celery and radishes calls for a vibrant, unoaked white wine that allows the flavor of the truffle to be the focal point of the dish. Terre di Franciacorta by Contaldi Castaldi is a northern Italian white that provides the ideal backdrop for the enticing aroma of the truffle. Christian Moreau's Chablis has the minerality to match with the potatoes and the preserved elements without suppressing other ingredients.

Salmon Roe–Potato Blini with Tobiko Wasabi Crème Fraîche and Osetra Caviar

Serves 4

These potato blini are as light as air and make a great foundation for showcasing one or several types of fish eggs. Salmon roe, which pops in the mouth, is folded into the blini batter, so the pleasant burst comes as a surprise. The crunchy, playfully spicy tobiko wasabi is served in the form of a rich sauce, which emphasizes the delicate nature of the barely warm blini. And finally — just to push things over the top — osetra caviar, with its hauntingly steely richness, sits like a king on his throne on top of it all. Extraordinary flavors and textures harmonize in a profound eating experience.

BLINI

1½ cups peeled and diced Yukon Gold potatoes, boiled and riced
½ cup flour
1 large egg
¼ cup milk
1 teaspoon baking powder
Salt and freshly ground black pepper
2 ounces salmon roe
2 tablespoons grapeseed oil

TOBIKO WASABI CRÈME FRAÎCHE

3 tablespoons crème fraîche
1 tablespoon (or more) heavy whipping cream
1 tablespoon vodka
3 tablespoons tobiko wasabi

GARNISH

2 ounces osetra caviar
4 tablespoons brunoise-cut hard-boiled egg white
2 tablespoons finely chopped fresh chives
2 tablespoons finely minced red onion
8 teaspoons Herb Oil *(see Appendices)*
¼ cup hard-boiled egg yolk, pressed through a fine-mesh sieve
1 teaspoon finely grated lemon zest
2 tablespoons very thinly diagonally cut scallion tops
Freshly ground black pepper

METHOD

To prepare the blini: Place the riced potatoes in a mixing bowl. Add the flour, egg, milk, and baking powder. Mix until the ingredients are thoroughly combined and the batter is smooth. Season with salt and pepper. Gently fold in the salmon roe. Preheat a nonstick sauté pan over medium-low heat. Coat the pan lightly with grapeseed oil. Spoon the batter by tablespoonfuls into the pan; cook for 3 to 4 minutes on each side, or until golden brown. Continue until there are at least 12 blini (the batter should yield extra blini for snacking along the way).

To prepare the wasabi crème fraîche: Place the crème fraîche, cream, and vodka in a mixing bowl; whisk together until smooth. If made ahead of time, the mixture will thicken; if this happens, add more cream. Fold in the tobiko wasabi just prior to use.

ASSEMBLY

At 3 parallel spots on each plate, spoon 1 teaspoon of the wasabi crème fraîche. Place a blin on top of each teaspoon of sauce and top each blin with a small quenelle of the osetra caviar. In a line behind the blini, sprinkle the egg white, chives, and red onion. Spoon the Herb Oil around the perimeter of the plate. Arrange the egg yolk in front of the blini in a horizontal line. Sprinkle the lemon zest and scallion pieces around the plate; top with pepper.

WINE NOTES

The richness of the potato blini requires a slightly fuller-bodied wine, but there are many delicate, subtle flavors in this dish that need a tender pairing. The sweetness and the fruity aromas of Alsatian Pinot Gris from Marcel Deiss contrast wonderfully with the salty osetra caviar without hiding its delicate flavor. The low acidity and rich midpalate of Divine Droplets sake also tie the elements of the dish together while reinforcing the Asian theme.

Mussel and Potato Soufflé with Curried Mussel Sauce

Serves 4

This preparation is whimsical and fun, as well as surprisingly easy to prepare.
Mussels and curry are already a superb combination, but here the pairing is elevated to glorious refinement.
If mussels do not appeal, try substituting crabmeat or chunks of Maine lobster. These soufflés make
an ideal start to a special dinner party; or a piece of poached fish can be placed next to each soufflé
to convert the preparation from starter to elegant entrée.

CURRIED MUSSEL SAUCE

2 shallots, chopped
3 cloves garlic, chopped
2 tablespoons chopped fresh ginger
1 stalk lemongrass, finely chopped
2 tablespoons extra virgin olive oil
1 tablespoon spicy Madras curry powder
2 tablespoons sweet curry powder
1 teaspoon ground cumin
½ cup tomato paste
3 cups water
½ cup loosely packed chopped fresh cilantro
10 mussels, cooked (unopened mussels discarded) and shelled
1 tablespoon freshly squeezed lime juice
Salt and freshly ground black pepper

SOUFFLÉS

1 cup egg whites (from about 6 large eggs)
4 ounces peeled, boiled, and riced Yukon Gold potato (about 1 potato)
2 large egg yolks
2 tablespoons flour
2 teaspoons cornstarch
¼ cup curried mussel sauce (above)
12 mussels, cooked (unopened mussels discarded) and shelled

GARNISH

20 mussels, cooked (unopened mussels discarded) and shelled
¼ cup chopped micro cilantro (or chopped fresh cilantro)
4 teaspoons Cilantro Oil *(see Appendices)*
Freshly ground black pepper

METHOD

To prepare the sauce: Sauté the shallots, garlic, ginger, and lemongrass in the olive oil over medium heat for 5 minutes, or until the shallots are translucent. Add both curry powders, the cumin, and the tomato paste; continue to cook for 2 minutes. Add the water and cilantro and cook for 10 more minutes. Transfer to a blender and purée until smooth. Pass through a fine-mesh sieve. Finely chop the mussels and fold into the sauce. Add the lime juice and season to taste with salt and pepper. Just prior to use, reheat if necessary.

To prepare the soufflés: Preheat the oven to 375°F. Butter and flour 4 individual soufflé dishes (about 3 inches in diameter and 3 inches high). In the bowl of an electric mixer fitted with the whisk attachment, whip the egg whites on medium speed to form stiff peaks, 3 to 4 minutes. Place the riced potato in a mixing bowl. Add the egg yolks, flour, and cornstarch to the potatoes; stir until fully incorporated. Fold in the ¼ cup curried mussel sauce until combined. Just prior to baking, fold in the whipped egg whites in three additions.

Fill each soufflé dish halfway with the soufflé batter. Place 3 mussels on top of the batter and top with more batter, leaving about ½ inch of space below the top of the dishes. Place the soufflé dishes in a roasting pan and add water to come halfway up the sides of the dishes. Bake for 20 minutes, or until the soufflés have risen and are golden brown. Loosen the sides of the soufflés with a knife; unmold the soufflés, then assemble and serve immediately.

ASSEMBLY

Place a soufflé in the center of each plate and spoon the sauce around the soufflé. Arrange 5 mussels around the plate and sprinkle with the micro cilantro. Spoon the Cilantro Oil around the plate and top with pepper.

WINE NOTES

The soufflé and the curried mussel sauce have a moderate level of fiery heat, which is combined with a taste of savory spices. Wines that are off-dry will downplay these dominant flavors. Gewürztraminer from Zind-Humbrecht's Goldert vineyard has a touch of sweetness and a low level of acidity that respond well to the airy soufflé. True to its name (*gewürz* means "spicy" in German), this wine also has the aromatics to complement the fragrance of the sauce.

Spiced Venison with Prune-Studded Potato Galette

Serves 4

*Though quite easy to execute, this memorable dish provides a complex interplay of flavors.
Venison tenderloin — or for that matter, any game bird — finds a superb accompaniment in the potato and prune galette.
The potato offers a soft, delicate earthiness, while the prunes lend a sophisticated sweetness
that cuts perfectly into the heady intensity of the meat. Crunchy celery and creamy potato purée add essential
textural notes that round out the sensual experience.*

PRUNE-STUDDED POTATO GALETTES
10 banana fingerling potatoes, thinly
 sliced into rings
⅓ cup butter, melted
½ cup finely grated Parmesan cheese
4 prunes, pitted and finely chopped
2 tablespoons water
Salt and freshly ground black pepper

POTATO PURÉE
1½ pounds Yukon Gold potatoes, peeled
 and chopped
1 cup milk, heated
½ cup butter
Salt and freshly ground black pepper

VENISON
2 teaspoons coriander seeds, toasted
 and crushed
½ teaspoon ground cinnamon
½ teaspoon ground star anise
⅛ teaspoon freshly ground black pepper
4 4-ounce medallions venison tenderloin
Salt
2 teaspoons grapeseed oil

CELERY
2 celery stalks, peeled and diagonally
 cut into ¼-inch-thick pieces
1 tablespoon butter
1 bay leaf
1 cup Chicken Stock *(see Appendices)*
1 sprig rosemary
1 tablespoon chopped fresh parsley
Salt and freshly ground black pepper

GARNISH
Pinch of ground cinnamon
⅛ teaspoon ground cumin
½ cup hot Meat Stock Reduction
 (see Appendices)
8 teaspoons Herb Oil *(see Appendices)*
4 teaspoons micro parsley
 (or chopped fresh parsley)

METHOD

To prepare the potato galettes: Preheat the oven to 350°F. Line a sheet pan with parchment paper. Using one-fourth of the potato slices, make eight 3-inch pinwheels. Brush the pinwheels with some of the melted butter and sprinkle lightly with some of the Parmesan cheese. Repeat this process until each pinwheel has at least 4 layers of potato. Transfer the wheels to the prepared sheet pan. Bake the potatoes for 30 to 35 minutes, or until the potatoes are tender and just turning golden brown.

In the meantime, place the prunes and water in a small saucepan and warm over medium heat. Season the prunes to taste with salt and pepper. Spread a ¼-inch-thick layer of the prunes over 4 of the potato wheels and cover the prunes with the remaining potato wheels.

To prepare the potato purée: Cook the potatoes in boiling salted water for 15 to 20 minutes, or until tender. Drain and pass through a ricer. Place in a medium bowl; add the milk and butter and whip until smooth. Season to taste with salt and pepper.

To prepare the venison: Combine all the spices. Season the venison with salt and rub the spices all over the venison. Heat a sauté pan over high heat. Add the grapeseed oil and the venison; cook for 5 minutes on each side, or until medium-rare. Remove the venison from the pan and let rest for 2 minutes before slicing the medallions in half.

To prepare the celery: Place the celery, butter, bay leaf, stock, and rosemary in a small saucepan; cook for 5 minutes over medium heat, or until the celery is bright green and al dente. Remove the bay leaf and rosemary and add the parsley. Season to taste with salt and pepper.

ASSEMBLY
Combine the cinnamon and cumin in a small bowl. Place an assembled potato galette off center on each plate. Spoon some of the celery pieces next to the potato and place 2 pieces of the venison atop the celery. Spoon the potato purée in a ring around the plate. Spoon the stock reduction over the venison and around the plate. Sprinkle just a pinch of the cinnamon-cumin mixture around the plate. Drizzle the Herb Oil around the celery and sprinkle with the micro parsley.

WINE NOTES
It's exciting to taste a wine from an unknown region and have it exceed all your expectations. Amphorae's Merlot from Galilee is almost Bordeaux-like with its notes of tobacco, vanilla, and plums. This wine has the body to match the richness of the venison and the potato purée while still having enough fruitiness to go with the prunes. The spice crust of the venison could dominate many wines, but the Amphorae is undaunted, responding with brown spice aromas of its own.

ROOT VEGETABLES

Serrano Ham and Phyllo–Wrapped Salsify with Bosc Pear and Caramelized Endive

Serves 4

In this simple but sophisticated recipe, crispy phyllo encases spears of sweet poached salsify wrapped in slices of richly satisfying serrano ham. Pieces of the phyllo rolls, along with braised Belgian endive, are then placed on a smear of satiny salsify purée to accentuate that extraordinary flavor. Slices of sautéed pear provide the perfect sweetness to contrast the bitter flavor of the endive and to cut into the rich and salty taste of the ham. A drizzle of a vinaigrette featuring raw endive and Asian pear provides the final emphasis on the bitter and sweet accents. Although this makes for a fine appetizer before a light entrée, slices of pork tenderloin or four or five shrimp could be added to fashion it into an entire meal.

SALSIFY

½ lemon, juiced
2 cups milk
6 stalks salsify
2 bay leaves
1 teaspoon peppercorns
3 sprigs thyme
Salt and freshly ground black pepper
6 sheets phyllo pastry
½ cup melted butter
¼ cup chopped fresh basil
¼ pound serrano ham, thinly sliced

ENDIVE

2 tablespoons butter
2 heads red Belgian endive, quartered
1 tablespoon sugar
½ cup water
Salt and freshly ground black pepper

PEAR

1 Bosc pear, cut into ⅛-inch-thick slices
1 tablespoon butter
Salt and freshly ground black pepper

VINAIGRETTE

1 shallot, minced
¼ cup small-diced Asian pear
2 tablespoons apple cider vinegar
6 tablespoons extra virgin olive oil
½ cup finely chopped red Belgian endive
1 tablespoon chopped fresh chives
Salt and freshly ground black pepper

GARNISH

¼ cup micro parsley (or chopped fresh parsley)
Freshly ground black pepper

METHOD

To prepare the salsify: Add the lemon juice and milk to a saucepan large enough that the salsify can lie flat. Peel the salsify and trim the ends. Immediately place the salsify in the pan, add water to cover, and add the bay leaves, peppercorns, and thyme. Bring the mixture to a slow simmer and cook for 10 to 15 minutes, or until the salsify is al dente. Remove the salsify from the liquid to prevent overcooking. Coarsely chop 2 of the salsify stalks (pick 2 that don't match the others in size) and place in a blender. Purée with just enough of the cooking liquid to make a smooth saucelike consistency. Just prior to serving, season the salsify purée to taste with salt and pepper and reheat.

Preheat the oven to 375°F. Line a sheet pan with parchment paper.

Lay 1 sheet of the phyllo on a flat work surface; brush lightly with some of the melted butter and sprinkle with some of the basil. Carefully lay 2 more sheets of phyllo atop the first, brushing each layer with some of the melted butter and sprinkling with the basil. Trim away any rough or dry edges and set aside. Repeat this process with the other 3 sheets of phyllo. Cover the lower half of each prepared phyllo stack with the serrano ham and lay 2 stalks of the salsify side by side over the ham on each stack. Carefully roll up the phyllo sheets like a cigar, secure with a light coating of the melted butter, and brush the outside layer of the rolls with the melted butter. Transfer the phyllo wraps to the parchment-lined sheet pan and bake for 20 minutes, or until golden brown and crispy. Carefully trim the ends of the phyllo and slice each diagonally into 4 pieces.

To prepare the endive: Melt the butter in a sauté pan over medium-high heat and add the endive, cut side down. Cook for 5 minutes on each side, or until caramelized. Add the sugar and water, cover, and continue to cook for 10 minutes, or until the endive is tender. Remove from the pan and season to taste with salt and pepper.

To prepare the pear: Sauté the pear slices in the butter over medium heat until golden brown, about 6 minutes. Season to taste with salt and pepper.

To prepare the vinaigrette: Place the shallot, pear, and vinegar in a small bowl and slowly whisk in the olive oil. Add the endive and chives and season to taste with salt and pepper.

ASSEMBLY

Spoon some of the salsify purée down the center of each plate. Place 2 endive quarters in the center of each plate and lay a few pear slices around the endive. Place 2 pieces of the phyllo-wrapped salsify atop the pears and drizzle the vinaigrette around the plate. Sprinkle with the micro parsley and top with pepper.

WINE NOTES

The richness of this full-flavored dish is cut slightly and lightened by the bitterness of the endive, the saltiness of the serrano ham, and the bright acid of a Jackson Estate Sauvignon Blanc. The passion fruit and grapefruit notes of this Marlborough Sauvignon Blanc are brightened by the dish and complement the pears.

Chicken with Salt-Crusted Heirloom Beets and Mustard Sauce

Serves 4

When these beets — which are tremendous on their own — are cooked in a salt crust, the result is magical. The flavor becomes more intense and complex, yet the beets stay quite moist; their natural sweetness and earthiness take on a remarkable refinement. Roast chicken — or even lamb or veal — complements the beets without taking center stage, and a playfully assertive sauce featuring whole grain mustard provides just the right bite, cutting superbly across the principal elements on the plate. By using only two or three slices of chicken and tossing everything with some greens and maybe Belgian endive, this dish could easily be coverted into a stunning salad.

BEETS

8 baby red beets
8 baby yellow beets
8 baby candy cane beets
8 sprigs thyme, stems removed
4 sprigs rosemary, stems removed
4 bay leaves
2 tablespoons extra virgin olive oil
4 large egg whites
¼ cup sea salt
1 teaspoon sherry wine vinegar
Salt and freshly ground black pepper

MUSTARD SAUCE

1 quart Chicken Stock *(see Appendices)*
1 tablespoon whole grain mustard
1 tablespoon butter, softened
1 teaspoon chopped fresh tarragon
Salt and freshly ground black pepper

CHICKEN

1 tablespoon extra virgin olive oil
4 small chicken breasts, skin on
Salt and freshly ground black pepper

GARNISH

Freshly ground black pepper
¼ cup micro parsley (or chopped
   fresh parsley)

METHOD

To prepare the beets: Preheat the oven to 400°F. Toss all the beets with the thyme, rosemary, bay leaves, and olive oil and place in an ovenproof pan. Whip the egg whites until stiff peaks form; fold in the salt and vinegar. Cover the beets with the egg white mixture and cover the pan with aluminum foil. Roast for 30 minutes. Remove from the oven and peel back the foil. The egg mixture should be hard, and it should be possible to lift it off in big pieces; do so and discard the egg mixture. Remove the beets and, using your hands, peel away their skins. Cut the beets in half and season to taste with salt and pepper.

To prepare the sauce: Simmer the stock in a saucepan over medium heat for 30 to 45 minutes, or until reduced to ½ cup. Remove from the heat and whisk in the mustard and butter. Fold in the tarragon. Season to taste with salt and pepper.

To prepare the chicken: Preheat the oven to 400°F. Heat the oil in an ovenproof sauté pan over high heat. Season the chicken with salt and pepper and place in the pan skin side down. Cook for 5 minutes, or until the skin is golden brown. Flip the chicken over and transfer the pan to the oven; cook for 10 minutes, or until the chicken is just cooked through. Remove the chicken from the pan and let rest for 3 minutes before slicing thinly. Season the sliced chicken to taste with salt and pepper.

ASSEMBLY

Arrange some of the beets on each plate. Lay some of the chicken slices over the beets and spoon the mustard sauce over the chicken and around the plate. Top with pepper and sprinkle with the micro parsley.

WINE NOTES

The heirloom beets and roasted chicken breast in this course caused even lightly oak-aged wines to taste bitter and over-oaked. Grosset's "Polish Hill" Riesling from the Clare Valley in South Australia—a dry, medium-bodied, aromatic white with vibrant acid—matched the stony flavors of the beets and also complemented the spice notes of the mustard sauce.

Curried Beef Short Ribs with Roasted Parsnip, Carrot, Rutabaga, and Potato

Serves 4

This entrée is composed of an utterly irresistible layering of flavors and textures. The braised root vegetables are like butter and practically disappear without chewing; the short ribs, hauntingly spiced with curry, provide just the right contrasting chewiness. Crunchy almonds and dried currants add simple yet profound flavor notes, and with a few finely julienned strands of kaffir lime leaf comes a burst of the surreal perfume of tropical citrus. And as if that isn't enough, this preparation actually tastes better on the second or third day after making it.

SHORT RIBS

2 tablespoons grapeseed oil
4 pounds beef short ribs
Salt and freshly ground black pepper
8 cloves garlic, smashed
3 red Thai chiles, minced
2 6-inch pieces fresh lemongrass, chopped
3 tablespoons minced fresh ginger
1 yellow onion, chopped
2 tablespoons sweet curry powder
2 cups Beef Stock *(see Appendices)*
1 cup unsweetened coconut milk

VEGETABLES

2 carrots, peeled and cut diagonally
  into 1-inch pieces
2 parsnips, peeled and cut diagonally
  into 1-inch pieces
1 rutabaga, peeled and cut into
  small wedges
20 pearl onions, peeled
8 fingerling potatoes, cut diagonally
  into 1-inch pieces
1 tablespoon grapeseed oil
2 sprigs thyme
1 sprig rosemary
3 kaffir lime leaves, torn
Salt and freshly ground black pepper

GARNISH

¼ cup sliced almonds
1 tablespoon black currants
1 kaffir lime leaf, finely shredded
¼ lime

METHOD

To prepare the short ribs: Preheat the oven to 300˚F. Heat the grapeseed oil in a roasting pan over high heat. Season the ribs with salt and pepper on both sides. Sear the ribs in the roasting pan for about 7 minutes on each side, or until golden brown. Transfer the ribs to a plate. Add the garlic, chiles, lemongrass, ginger, and onion to the same pan; lower the heat to medium and cook until fragrant, about 3 minutes. Stir in the curry powder, then add the stock, coconut milk, and seared ribs. Cover the pan with a tight-fitting lid and cook in the oven for 5 hours, or until the ribs are extremely tender.

To prepare the vegetables: Toss the root vegetables, oil, herbs, and kaffir lime leaves together and place in another roasting pan. Season with salt and pepper. Cover and roast at 300˚F for 1 hour, or until tender.

ASSEMBLY

Remove the bones from the short ribs. Place the meat and vegetables in the center of 4 wide, shallow bowls. Ladle the braising liquid from the short ribs into each bowl and garnish with the almonds, currants, and kaffir lime leaf. Squeeze the lime over the top.

WINE NOTES

Beef short ribs are full-flavored, well-marbled meats that are predominantly paired with massive, full-bodied red wines. This dish, however, is an exception: the considerable spiciness from the curry sauce distorts the flavor of such bottlings, diluting the fruit in the wine while intensifying the heat of the alcohol. Rich, voluptuous white wines with a medium level of sweetness control the effect of the piquant curry sauce. Clos Saint Imer Pinot Gris from the Goldert vineyard in Alsace is a good choice because it also has the body to stand up to the short ribs.

Five Spice–Crusted Tuna with Roasted Carrots and Rutabaga Purée

Serves 4

Here the full flavor of the meaty tuna is given new complexity with a dusting of spices before the fish is seared.
The slowly roasted baby carrots, along with rutabaga, leeks, and pearl onions, add just the right concentrated sweetness to counter
the ethereal blend of spices; and they have a touch of earthiness that stands up well to the meatiness of the tuna.
In all, the flavors provide an extraordinary balance between sophistication and heartiness—ideal for a chilly autumn night.

ROASTED CARROTS AND RUTABAGA PURÉE

4 baby yellow carrots, peeled
4 baby orange carrots, peeled
4 baby red carrots, peeled
8 pearl onions, peeled
1 small rutabaga, cut into small wedges
8 baby leeks, cleaned
1 cinnamon stick
3 whole cloves
6 whole allspice berries
4 whole star anise
1 teaspoon pink peppercorns
2 tablespoons extra virgin olive oil
Salt and freshly ground black pepper
¼ cup Roasted Garlic *(see Appendices)*
1 cup Vegetable Stock *(see Appendices)*

TUNA

2 8-ounce bigeye tuna pieces (5 inches
   long and 1½ inches square)
Salt and freshly ground black pepper
¼ teaspoon ground cinnamon
¼ teaspoon ground star anise
¼ teaspoon ground cloves
¼ teaspoon ground allspice
¼ teaspoon pink peppercorns, crushed
1 tablespoon grapeseed oil

GARNISH

4 teaspoons chopped fresh chives
Freshly ground black pepper

METHOD

To prepare the roasted carrots and rutabaga purée: Preheat the oven to 300°F. Place all the carrots, the pearl onions, rutabaga, leeks, whole spices, and olive oil in a roasting pan. Toss together, season with salt and pepper, and cover. Cook for 3 hours, or until the vegetables are tender. Remove half of the rutabaga from the pan and place in a blender with the garlic and stock. Purée until smooth and season to taste with salt and pepper. Reheat the purée if necessary just prior to use. Remove the whole spices before serving the vegetables.

To prepare the tuna: Season the tuna with salt and pepper. Combine all the spices in a small bowl and sprinkle lightly on all sides of the tuna. Heat the grapeseed oil in a sauté pan over high heat. Sear the tuna in the oil for 1 minute on each side, or until golden brown on the outside and rare inside. Remove the tuna pieces from the pan and slice each into 4 thick pieces.

ASSEMBLY

Spoon the rutabaga purée in a zigzag on each plate. Cascade the vegetables down one side, and place 2 pieces of the tuna on the other side. Sprinkle with the chives and top with pepper.

WINE NOTES

This preparation can be paired with a California Pinot Noir or a white Burgundy—or, depending on your mood, both! The Littorai Pinot from the Hirsch Vineyard on the Sonoma coast has a wealth of sweet spices that enhance the spice-encrusted tuna, as well as fruity aromas to contrast with the roasted carrots. Jean-Philippe Fichet's Meursault "Les Chevalières" is a crisp version of Meursault, with zippy acidity and a medium body that doesn't overwhelm the tuna.

Bison with Root Vegetable Pavé and Parsnip Purée

Serves 4

Although this preparation is relatively straightforward, the result is both elegant and soul satisfying. A bite of the pavé melts in the mouth with the distinctive and subtle flavors of the root vegetables, and the bison tenderloin is a special treat indeed (though beef or chicken, or even tuna or lobster, can easily be substituted). A pool of very loose parsnip purée brings a glorious creaminess to the plate, and a small drizzle of intense meat jus is all that is required to complete this very regal dish.

PAVÉ

1 celery root, peeled and thinly sliced
4 carrots, peeled and thinly sliced
1 rutabaga, peeled and thinly sliced
4 parsnips, peeled and thinly sliced
1 sweet potato, peeled and thinly sliced
5 cups heavy whipping cream
2 tablespoons butter, melted
Salt and freshly ground black pepper

PARSNIP PURÉE

½ cup chopped peeled parsnip
½ cup milk
Salt and freshly ground black pepper

BISON

1 tablespoon grapeseed oil
4 6-ounce bison tenderloin pieces
Salt and freshly ground black pepper

GARNISH

1 cup hot Meat Stock Reduction
  (see Appendices)
2 teaspoons fresh rosemary leaves
4 teaspoons extra virgin olive oil

METHOD

To prepare the pavé: Preheat the oven to 350°F. Place the vegetable slices in 5 separate bowls. Add 1 cup of the cream to each bowl and toss gently to coat the slices evenly. Line an 8-inch-square pan with aluminum foil and brush the foil with ½ tablespoon of the melted butter. Arrange a layer of the celery root slices in the bottom of the pan, overlapping them slightly, and lightly season with salt and pepper. Arrange a layer of the carrot slices on top of the celery root, overlapping them slightly, and lightly season with salt and pepper. Continue to layer with the rutabaga, parsnips, and sweet potato. Continue alternating layers until all the vegetables are used. Cover the pan tightly with a second sheet of aluminum foil brushed with ½ tablespoon of the butter. Place another 8-inch-square pan over the foil and weigh it down with a brick or other heavy ovenproof object. Bake for 2½ hours, or until the root vegetables are tender. Leaving the weight on the pan, refrigerate the pavé for at least 4 hours and up to 1 day.

Remove the pavé from the refrigerator. Remove the weight, the top pan, and the foil, and invert the pavé onto a sheet pan. Remove the foil and cut out four 2-inch squares (the remaining pavé will keep in the refrigerator for several days). Heat the remaining 1 tablespoon butter in a large nonstick sauté pan over medium-high heat. Add the pavé squares and cook for 3 to 4 minutes, or until golden brown. Carefully turn the pavé squares and cook for 3 to 4 minutes, or until warmed through. (If the pavé is still not warm in the middle, it can be heated in a 375°F oven for 5 minutes.)

To prepare the parsnip purée: Cook the chopped parsnip in the milk over medium-low heat for 10 minutes, or until the parsnip is tender. Purée the parsnip with enough of the milk to make a smooth consistency. Season to taste with salt and pepper.

To prepare the bison: Prepare a medium-hot grill. Brush the grapeseed oil over the bison and season with salt and pepper. Grill the bison for 5 to 7 minutes on each side, or until medium-rare. Remove from the grill and let rest for 3 minutes. Trim the ends and slice each tenderloin piece into 3 pieces. Season the sliced meat to taste with salt and pepper.

ASSEMBLY

Spoon some of the parsnip purée in the center of each plate. Place a piece of the pavé just left of center on each plate and arrange the sliced bison in the center. Spoon the stock reduction over the bison and around the plate. Sprinkle with the rosemary leaves and drizzle the olive oil around the plate.

WINE NOTES

Cabernet Franc-based wines, such as Saumur-Champigny from the Loire Valley or Sirita from the Napa Valley, succeed in stressing the earthy notes of the pavé. The fuller-bodied Sirita rounds out the dish, while the Cabernet Franc from the Loire has a higher level of acidity that cleanses the palate. Château de Villeneuve and Clos Rougeard both produce great examples of Saumur-Champigny.

Lobster and Yellow Beet Borscht with Frozen Dill-Mascarpone Cream

Serves 4

*This interpretation of borscht is satiny and earthy, yet at the same time quite delicate.
Slices of lobster meat add richness, and a scoop of frozen dill-mascarpone cream makes the perfect texture and flavor
foil to the other elements in this dish. Pieces of heart of palm provide a final note of whimsy.*

BORSCHT

5 medium yellow beets
½ cup water
3 bay leaves
1 clove garlic, crushed
2 tablespoons extra virgin olive oil
1 whole star anise
2 whole cloves
Salt and freshly ground black pepper
3 cups Vegetable Stock *(see Appendices)*

GARNISH

8 baby red beets
3 tablespoons extra virgin olive oil
3 tablespoons 1-inch sprigs fresh dill
3 lobster tails, cooked and sliced into
    20 medallions total
1 teaspoon freshly squeezed lemon juice
Salt and freshly ground black pepper
½ cup diagonally sliced heart of palm
1 tablespoon prepared horseradish

FROZEN DILL-MASCARPONE CREAM

1 cup firmly packed dill sprigs
½ cup crème fraîche
1 cup mascarpone cheese
1 tablespoon freshly squeezed lime juice
¼ cup prepared horseradish
Salt and freshly ground black pepper

METHOD

To prepare the borscht: Preheat the oven to 350°F. Place the beets, water, bay leaves, garlic, 1 tablespoon of the olive oil, the star anise, and cloves in a roasting pan. Season with salt and pepper and cover the pan with aluminum foil. Roast for 1½ hours, or until the beets are tender. Peel the beets and chop coarsely. Purée the beets in a blender with the stock and the remaining 1 tablespoon olive oil. Season to taste with salt and pepper. Refrigerate until ready to use.

To prepare the garnish: Place the red beets and 1 tablespoon of the olive oil in a roasting pan and cook in a 350°F oven for 45 minutes, or until tender. Peel the beets and slice them into sixths. Chop 1 tablespoon of the dill sprigs and place in a small bowl with the lobster, lemon juice, and 1 tablespoon of the olive oil; season to taste with salt and pepper. In another bowl, toss the heart of palm with the horseradish and season to taste with salt and pepper.

To prepare the mascarpone cream: Purée the dill and crème fraîche in a blender until smooth; pass though a sieve into a mixing bowl. Fold in the mascarpone, lime juice, and horseradish. Season to taste with salt and pepper and place in the freezer for 1 hour, or until firm but not frozen solid.

ASSEMBLY

Ladle the borscht into 4 shallow bowls. Arrange some of the heart of palm mixture in the center of the soup and place 5 lobster pieces around the bowl. Place some of the red beets in the bowl. Drizzle the remaining 1 tablespoon olive oil around the soup and place a quenelle-shaped piece of the mascarpone cream atop the heart of palm. Sprinkle with the remaining 2 tablespoons dill and freshly ground black pepper.

WINE NOTES

Chablis from Raveneau is a pure expression of the soil and the Chardonnay grape, without the interference of oak. Raveneau's "Les Clos" and "Montée de Tonnerre" are intellectual wines that do not have the obviousness of most California Chardonnays. Their bright mineral tastes are a wonderful supplement to the lobster and yellow beets in the borscht. The cool climate of Chablis gives these wines an intense acid backbone.

SQUASH

Venison with Cardamom-Flavored Butternut Squash and Red Wine–Date Sauce

Serves 4

A rich, full-flavored piece of meat like venison benefits tremendously from a pairing that offers just a touch of sweetness, like butternut squash. Here the squash gains complexity from the addition of cardamom and Thai chiles. A spirited red wine–date sauce complements and contrasts with both the meat and the squash, and pearl onions braised in chicken stock round out the presentation. Pork or duck would make fine substitutions for the venison.

SQUASH
1 small butternut squash, halved and
   seeds removed
2 teaspoons extra virgin olive oil
1 teaspoon fresh thyme leaves
2 teaspoons ground cardamom
2 dried Thai chiles, crushed
Salt and freshly ground black pepper
1 cup water
2 tablespoons butter, softened

PEARL ONIONS
20 pearl onions, blanched and peeled
2 cups Chicken Stock *(see Appendices)*
1 tablespoon chopped fresh flat-leaf parsley
Salt and freshly ground black pepper

RED WINE–DATE SAUCE
6 dates, pitted and cut into sixths
½ cup Red Wine Reduction
   (see Appendices)
½ cup Meat Stock Reduction
   (see Appendices)

VENISON
1 tablespoon grapeseed oil
4 4-ounce medallions venison tenderloin
Salt and freshly ground black pepper
2 tablespoons chopped fresh sage

GARNISH
6 chives, cut diagonally into 1-inch pieces
Freshly ground black pepper

METHOD
To prepare the squash: Preheat the oven to 350°F. Rub the inside of the squash with the olive oil, thyme, cardamom, and chiles. Season with salt and pepper and place cut side down on a rimmed sheet pan. Add the water to the sheet pan and cook for 1½ hours, or until the squash is tender. Scrape the pulp from the squash skins and pass the pulp through a food mill. Fold in the butter and season to taste with salt and pepper.

To prepare the onions: Place the onions in a sauté pan with the stock and cook over medium heat until the onions are caramelized and the stock is almost completely gone, about 40 minutes. Add the parsley and season to taste with salt and pepper.

To prepare the sauce: Combine all the ingredients in a saucepan and bring to a simmer.

To prepare the venison: Heat the grapeseed oil in a sauté pan over high heat. Season the venison with salt and pepper, sprinkle with the sage, and add to the pan. Cook for 5 minutes on each side, or until medium-rare.

ASSEMBLY
Spoon some of the squash in the center of each plate and place a piece of the venison atop the squash. Place some of the pearl onions around the venison. Spoon the date sauce over the venison and around the plate. Sprinkle with the chives and top with pepper.

WINE NOTES
German Riesling and venison? This could become a new classic combination. The venison isn't the most important element here; its impact is mitigated by the semisweet red wine–date sauce and the roasted butternut squash purée. But these sweet elements cause many wines to taste sour and biting. The gentle sweetness of JJ Prüm's Wehlener Sonnenuhr Riesling Auslese is the perfect match for those components, and isn't overwhelmed by the venison.

Asparagus and Zucchini Soup with Crayfish

Serves 4

This dish, while very light and delicate, is packed with flavor. After a light grilling, zucchini and asparagus are blended together with water and olive oil to create a vibrant soup. Crayfish provide a sensual richness that becomes powerfully evident when contrasted with the subtle flavor of the soup. Tiny asparagus pieces add not only important flavor notes but textural elements as well. A drizzle of Shellfish Oil to finish further highlights the glorious flavor of the sweet crayfish.

SOUP

20 asparagus stalks, trimmed
2 zucchini, quartered lengthwise
2 tablespoons extra virgin olive oil
Salt and freshly ground black pepper
3 cups water
½ lemon, juiced

CRAYFISH

2 tablespoons minced shallot
2 teaspoons minced garlic
1 tablespoon extra virgin olive oil
8 baby zucchini, thinly sliced diagonally
8 pattypan squash, quartered
½ cucumber, peeled, seeded, and cut
    into small wedges
32 crayfish, peeled
Grilled asparagus tips (above)
1 tablespoon freshly squeezed lemon juice
½ cup Pinot Gris
Salt and freshly ground black pepper

GARNISH

4 teaspoons Shellfish Oil
    (see Appendices)
1 tablespoon chopped fresh
    flat-leaf parsley
Freshly ground black pepper

METHOD

To prepare the soup: Prepare a medium-hot grill. Toss the asparagus and zucchini with 1 tablespoon of the olive oil and season with salt and pepper. Place the vegetables over a moderate flame on the grill. Cook for 3 to 5 minutes, or until tender. Trim the tips from the asparagus and reserve for the crayfish mixture. Chop the remaining asparagus and place in a blender with the zucchini, water, lemon juice, and the remaining 1 tablespoon olive oil. Purée until smooth. Season the soup to taste with salt and pepper. Pass through a medium sieve if fibrous. Warm the soup just prior to serving.

To prepare the crayfish: Sauté the shallot and garlic in the olive oil over medium heat until translucent, about 5 minutes. Add the zucchini, pattypan squash, and cucumber; cook for 5 minutes. Add the crayfish, reserved asparagus tips, lemon juice, and wine; continue to cook for 3 minutes, or until the vegetables are tender. Season to taste with salt and pepper.

ASSEMBLY

Arrange some of the crayfish mixture in the center of each bowl and carefully ladle in the soup around the mixture. Drizzle the Shellfish Oil around the soup and sprinkle with the chopped parsley. Top with pepper.

WINE NOTES

Some exciting Rieslings are starting to be produced in the Willamette Valley of Oregon in addition to the topflight Pinot Noirs. Brooks Riesling, a 100 percent biodynamic wine, has bright mineral notes that push the flavor of the crayfish to the forefront. This cool-climate Riesling also has fresh acidity that keeps the flavors in this dish lively and vibrant.

Beef and Barley Soup
with Roasted Red Kuri Squash

Serves 4

This is a great make-ahead preparation that can be heated at the last moment and served up with ease.
It's fun to use the squash rind as a bowl for the stew; this allows for combining mouthfuls of the delectable, complexly flavored
roasted squash with bites of the soup. Lamb or venison would stand in nicely for the beef.

SQUASH

4 small Red Kuri squash (about the size
  of a grapefruit)
2 tablespoons extra virgin olive oil
4 bay leaves
4 sprigs thyme
4 sprigs rosemary
4 1-inch pieces fresh ginger, peeled
Salt and freshly ground black pepper

SOUP

1 tablespoon grapeseed oil
1½ pounds beef stew meat,
  cut into ½-inch dice
Salt and freshly ground black pepper
1 red onion, cut into small dice
2 cloves garlic, minced
10 brussels sprouts, halved
3 cups Beef Stock *(see Appendices)*
2 whole star anise
1 tablespoon maple sugar
1 tablespoon sherry wine vinegar
2 tablespoons butter
3 cups cooked pearl barley, hot
2 tablespoons chopped fresh flat-leaf parsley
1 tablespoon chopped fresh chives
Diced cooked squash from squash tops
  (above)

METHOD

To prepare the squash: Preheat the oven to 350˚F. Cut the top one-third off each squash. Scrape out the seeds and rub the insides of the tops and bottoms with the olive oil. Place 1 bay leaf, a sprig of thyme, a sprig of rosemary, and a piece of ginger in each squash bottom and season the inside with salt and pepper. Put the tops back on and place in an ovenproof pan. Roast the squash for 1 to 1½ hours, or until tender. Remove the herbs and ginger from the squash. Cut the pulp out of the squash tops; cut into a medium dice and set aside. Reserve the squash bottoms. The squash bottoms may need to be reheated just prior to serving.

To prepare the soup: Heat the grapeseed oil in a large saucepan over high heat. Season the beef with salt and pepper. Add to the pan and sear until golden brown. Add the onion, garlic, and brussels sprouts. Cook for 7 to 10 minutes, or until the onion is caramelized. Add the stock, star anise, maple sugar, and vinegar; cook over low heat for 15 minutes. Add the butter and barley to the pan; stir until combined. Fold in the chopped herbs and the reserved diced squash and season to taste with salt and pepper.

ASSEMBLY

Place a squash bottom in the center of each shallow bowl. Fill the squash with the beef and barley soup and top with freshly ground black pepper.

WINE NOTES

The plethora of earthy, roasted flavors in this soup match perfectly with the rustic Syrahs of Cornas. Alain Voge and Auguste Clape produce two of the finest examples from the region. The tannin and structure of these wines compete with the barley and beef for dominance on the palate; neither side wins, but the struggle provides certain entertainment for the taste buds. The black pepper and spice from the Syrah grapes are also enhanced by the roasted squash.

Lobster with Hokkaido Squash Soup and Brown Butter

Serves 4

*Lobster and squash are already a superb combination, but this interpretation,
with its textural and flavor notes of citrus, apple, and watercress, reaches a higher level. Peppery watercress
provides a magnificent contrast, cutting through the sweeter components. Star anise is lightly dusted
over the lobster meat and soup for just the right hint of exoticism.*

SOUP

1 Hokkaido squash, halved and
   seeds removed
1 tablespoon extra virgin olive oil
1 teaspoon ground star anise
Salt and freshly ground black pepper
3 cups water
1 cup freshly squeezed orange juice
1 tablespoon rice wine vinegar
1 tablespoon butter

BROWN BUTTER

¾ cup butter

LOBSTER

4 small lobster tails, cooked and cut
   into ⅓-inch-thick medallions
1½ tablespoons brown butter (above)
Salt and freshly ground black pepper

GARNISH

24 stems watercress, thick stems
   trimmed away
Salt and freshly ground black pepper
1 cup small-diced water chestnuts
2 tablespoons small-diced Granny Smith
   apple
1 orange, peeled, supremed, and
   segments cut into thirds
1 tablespoon finely grated orange zest
¼ teaspoon ground star anise

METHOD

To prepare the soup: Preheat the oven to 375°F. Rub the inside of the squash with the olive oil and star anise; season with salt and pepper. Place cut side down in an ovenproof pan and add 1 cup of the water. Roast the squash for 1½ hours, or until tender. Remove the pulp from the skin and purée the pulp in a blender with the remaining 2 cups water, the orange juice, and the vinegar until smooth. If the soup is too thick, add additional orange juice and water. Transfer the soup to a saucepan and warm over medium heat; whisk in the butter and season to taste with salt and pepper.

To prepare the brown butter: Place the butter in a small saucepan and melt over medium-low heat. Continue to simmer the butter slowly, allowing the milk solids to rise to the top. Skim off the milk solids. Once the butter has a nutty aroma and dark brown specks in the bottom of the pan, it is ready to use.

To prepare the lobster: Preheat the oven to 400°F. Lay the lobster medallions flat in an ovenproof pan; drizzle with 1½ tablespoons of the brown butter and season with salt and pepper. Place in the oven for 2 minutes, or until just hot. Remove the lobster from the pan and reserve the juices in the pan.

ASSEMBLY

Toss the watercress in the reserved lobster juices; season to taste with salt and pepper. In the center of each shallow bowl, arrange some of the water chestnuts, apple, and watercress (reserve 8 stems of the watercress). Divide the lobster among the 4 bowls and arrange in an overlapping row atop the watercress. Sprinkle the orange segments around the bowl. Carefully pour some of the soup into each bowl around the lobster. Drizzle some of the brown butter over the lobster and around the soup. Sprinkle the orange zest and star anise over the soup and lobster and arrange the reserved watercress over the lobster.

WINE NOTES

The Hokkaido squash soup is rich with a low level of acidity, and is accented by an apple and orange garnish. The full-bodied Cuvée Sainte Catherine Riesling from Domaine Weinbach has lively acidity that cuts through the brown butter and reveals the citrus notes. A Pinot Blanc from Chalone accentuates the spice notes and makes another stellar pairing.

Buttermilk-Poached Pheasant Breast with Blue Hubbard Squash–Strewn Quinoa and Pumpkin Seed Oil

Serves 4

Although this dish has earthy overtones, it is nevertheless quite ethereal.
Meltingly soft pheasant breast that has been poached in buttermilk sits atop a mound of quinoa studded
with dried cherries and pepitas. Chunks of blue Hubbard squash, along with its purée,
encircle the bird and the grain. Spiced roasted pepitas and pumpkin seed oil, along with sprouts, complete the ensemble.
Conveniently, everything can be prepared in advance and then heated up at the last moment.

SQUASH

1 blue Hubbard squash, halved and
  seeds removed
2 tablespoons butter
½ teaspoon chili powder
1 teaspoon fresh thyme leaves
1½ cups Vegetable Stock *(see Appendices)*
Salt and freshly ground black pepper

SPICED PEPITAS

¾ cup pepitas (pumpkin seeds)
¼ teaspoon chili powder
¼ teaspoon Hungarian sweet paprika
1 teaspoon sugar
1½ tablespoons extra virgin olive oil
Salt and freshly ground black pepper

PHEASANT

2 pheasant breasts, skin removed
1 clove garlic, crushed
1 bay leaf
3 sprigs thyme
2 cups buttermilk
1 tablespoon extra virgin olive oil
1 tablespoon chopped micro tatsoi sprouts
  (or chopped fresh flat-leaf parsley)
Salt and freshly ground black pepper

QUINOA

2 teaspoons extra virgin olive oil
1 teaspoon minced fresh ginger
¼ cup minced shallot
2 cups cooked quinoa
¼ cup chopped dried sweet cherries
½ cup spiced pepitas (above)
1 cup cooked squash wedges (above)
2 tablespoons chopped fresh chives
1 tablespoon pumpkin seed oil
1 tablespoon balsamic vinegar
Salt and freshly ground black pepper

GARNISH

4 teaspoons pumpkin seed oil
2 tablespoons micro tatsoi sprouts

METHOD

To prepare the squash: Cut the squash into 1-inch wedges. Place in a large sauté pan with the butter and cook over medium heat for 10 minutes. Add the chili powder and thyme and continue to cook until the squash is caramelized and tender, about 5 minutes. Reserve 2 cups of the squash wedges and reheat before serving if necessary. Purée the remaining squash in a blender with the stock until smooth, then pass through a fine-mesh sieve. Warm the squash purée in a small saucepan and season to taste with salt and pepper.

To prepare the pepitas: Preheat the oven to 400°F. Line a sheet pan with parchment paper. Combine the pepitas, chili powder, paprika, sugar, and olive oil in a bowl and season with salt and pepper. Spread out on the parchment-lined sheet pan and bake for 7 minutes, or until toasted.

To prepare the pheasant: Place the pheasant, garlic, bay leaf, thyme, and buttermilk in a shallow saucepan and bring to a slow simmer. Simmer the pheasant for 20 minutes, or until just cooked through. Remove the pheasant from the buttermilk and let rest for 3 minutes before cutting into ⅓-inch-thick slices. Gently toss the slices with the olive oil and chopped tatsoi sprouts, and season to taste with salt and pepper.

To prepare the quinoa: Place the olive oil, ginger, and shallots in a sauté pan and cook over medium heat until the shallots are translucent, about 5 minutes. Add the quinoa, cherries, pepitas, and 1 cup of the reserved squash wedges. Once combined, add the chives, pumpkin seed oil, and balsamic vinegar; season to taste with salt and pepper.

ASSEMBLY

Place a 5-inch ring mold in the center of each plate; fill ½ inch high with the quinoa mixture and pack down firmly. Remove the ring mold and arrange 4 or 5 slices of the pheasant atop the quinoa mixture. Spoon the squash purée around the quinoa and place 5 or 6 of the reserved squash wedges around the sauce. Sprinkle the remaining pepitas around the plate and drizzle the pumpkin seed oil around the squash purée. Sprinkle with the micro tatsoi sprouts.

WINE NOTES

Along with some of the finest Cabernet Sauvignon vines in Napa, Robert Mondavi's To Kalon Vineyard also has excellent Sauvignon Blanc. The subtle oak aging of the To Kalon Fumé Blanc adds spice and nutty notes that complement the pumpkin seed oil and the pepitas. The intense citrus notes and acidity of the wine are a superb contrast to the roasted flavor of the pheasant.

Duck Confit and Zucchini Gratin with Hazelnut Vinaigrette and Red Wine Reduction

Serves 4

There is no question that this gratin fits squarely in the comfort-food category, but it's not overwhelmingly rich, and the portion size can be adjusted if just a small taste is desired. If you serve the complete recipe, you won't need much more to make a meal— a simple salad to start, and perhaps just fresh fruit for dessert.

DUCK CONFIT AND ZUCCHINI GRATIN

3 legs Duck Confit *(see Appendices)*
1 yellow onion, julienned
1 tablespoon butter
Salt and freshly ground black pepper
2 zucchini, thinly sliced into disks
2 cups grated yellow sharp
   Cheddar cheese

HAZELNUT VINAIGRETTE

2 tablespoons extra virgin olive oil
1 tablespoon hazelnut oil
2 tablespoons chopped toasted hazelnuts
1 tablespoon sherry wine vinegar
1 teaspoon balsamic vinegar
Salt and freshly ground black pepper

GARNISH

4 teaspoons Herb Oil *(see Appendices)*
¼ cup Red Wine Reduction
   (see Appendices), hot
¼ cup micro parsley sprouts (or chopped
   fresh flat-leaf parsley)
Freshly ground black pepper
⅛ teaspoon fleur de sel

METHOD

To prepare the gratins: Discard the skin and bones from the duck confit and shred the meat. Place the onion and butter in a sauté pan and cook over medium heat for 20 to 30 minutes, or until the onion is golden brown. Season to taste with salt and pepper. Preheat the oven to 400°F. Place four 5-inch-diameter by 2-inch-high ring molds on a sheet pan lined with parchment paper. Place a layer of zucchini in the bottom of each mold in a pinwheel pattern and lightly sprinkle with the cheese. Add a thin layer of the onion and a layer of the duck confit. Place a second layer of zucchini over the duck confit and continue to layer with the cheese, onions, duck confit, and zucchini until each mold is filled, ending with a layer of cheese. Transfer the sheet pan to the oven and bake for 10 to 15 minutes, or until the cheese is melted and beginning to turn golden brown. Carefully remove the molds.

To prepare the vinaigrette: Whisk together both oils, the nuts, and both vinegars; season to taste with salt and pepper.

ASSEMBLY

Place 1 gratin in the center of each plate. Spoon the hazelnut vinaigrette, Herb Oil, and wine reduction around the gratin. Sprinkle with the micro parsley sprouts and top with pepper and the fleur de sel.

WINE NOTES

The red wines of the Loire Valley are often overlooked, even though they offer tremendous flexibility in pairing with food. Charles Joguet is one of the top producers of Chinon, a lighter-bodied Cabernet Franc–based wine. The high acid of Cuvée Terroir provided a pleasing counterpoint to the Cheddar cheese and the duck confit. The earthy flavors of the gratin and the Chinon complemented each other and allowed the cranberry and plum notes of the wine to stand out.

TOMATOES

Braised Short Ribs with Tender Gnocchi and Tomato-Saffron Sauce

Serves 4

This dish is the ultimate in satisfying, hearty fare. The short ribs melt away in your mouth, as does the gnocchi; both are marvelously complemented by the heady and invigorating tomato-saffron sauce. Wilted collard greens or steamed haricots verts would be perfect served alongside.

SHORT RIBS

2 tablespoons grapeseed oil
4 beef short ribs, excess fat trimmed
Salt and freshly ground black pepper
1 cup chopped yellow onion
1 cup chopped leek
2 cups red tomatoes, chopped
12 cloves garlic, peeled
2 jalapeño chiles, halved
1½ cups red wine
2 sprigs rosemary
2 sprigs oregano
8 leaves fresh basil
1½ cups Chicken Stock *(see Appendices)*

TOMATO-SAFFRON SAUCE

2 tablespoons extra virgin olive oil
1 small yellow onion, finely chopped
4 cloves garlic, crushed
5 yellow tomatoes, peeled, seeded,
  and coarsely chopped
¼ cup chopped celery
¼ cup chopped peeled carrot
2 sprigs thyme
2 bay leaves
½ teaspoon lightly crushed saffron threads
2 tablespoons balsamic vinegar
Salt and freshly ground black pepper

GNOCCHI

2½ pounds baked, peeled, and riced russet
  potatoes (about 3 large potatoes), hot
1 egg
1 teaspoon salt
1 to 1½ cups flour
1 teaspoon butter
2 tablespoons chopped fresh basil
Salt and freshly ground black pepper

GARNISH

¼ cup globe basil leaves or micro basil
4 teaspoons extra virgin olive oil

METHOD

To prepare the short ribs: Preheat the oven to 300°F. Heat the grapeseed oil in a roasting pan over medium-high heat. Season the ribs with salt and pepper. Add the ribs to the pan and sear for 2 to 3 minutes on each side, or until golden brown. Remove the ribs from the pan and set aside. Add the onion and leek to the roasting pan and cook over medium heat for 7 to 10 minutes, or until golden brown. Add the tomatoes, garlic, and chiles; cook for 5 minutes, stirring to incorporate. Add the wine, rosemary, oregano, basil, and stock; bring to a simmer. Return the ribs to the pan and cover tightly with a lid or aluminum foil. Braise in the oven for 4 to 6 hours, or until the meat is fork-tender. (The braising liquid may be strained and reduced for use as a sauce, if desired.)

To prepare the tomato-saffron sauce: Place the olive oil and onion in a saucepan and cook over medium heat for 10 minutes, or until the onion is translucent. Add the garlic and cook for 3 more minutes. Add the tomatoes, celery, carrot, thyme, and bay leaves. Continue to cook over medium heat for 20 minutes, stirring occasionally. Add the saffron and balsamic vinegar and cook for 7 minutes over low heat. Cool slightly and purée in a blender until smooth. Season to taste with salt and pepper. Reheat if necessary before serving.

To prepare the gnocchi: Place the hot riced potatoes in a large bowl. Work the egg, salt, and ½ cup of the flour into the potatoes with a wooden spoon. Knead in enough of the remaining flour to form a silky, soft dough. Divide the dough into 4 equal portions and roll each portion into a long cigar shape about ½ inch in diameter. Cut the rolls into ½-inch pieces and gently pinch each piece in the center. Refrigerate on a lightly floured sheet pan until ready to cook.

Just before serving, poach the gnocchi in boiling salted water for 2 to 3 minutes, or just until they float. Transfer the gnocchi to a large bowl with a slotted spoon. Toss with the butter and basil; season to taste with salt and pepper. Serve immediately.

ASSEMBLY

Spoon a large circle of the tomato-saffron sauce into the center of each plate. Remove the short-rib meat from the bones and place a few pieces of meat in the center of each plate. Arrange the gnocchi around the meat. Sprinkle with the basil and spoon the olive oil around the plate.

WINE NOTES

Before tasting this course, one would think a full-bodied red wine would be the ideal pairing for the weight of the short ribs and gnocchi. This would be true were it not for the tomato-saffron sauce, which makes reds taste harsh and metallic; in turn, the wines completely bury the saffron aroma. Full-bodied Alsatian Riesling, however, works exceptionally well with the dish (no, I'm not crazy!). A Zind-Humbrecht Riesling from the Brand vineyard stands up to the rich, fatty short ribs while highlighting the tomato and saffron.

Soft-Shell Crab with Curried Tomato Sauce and Cumin Vinaigrette

Serves 4

This curried tomato sauce is a stellar accompaniment to the soft-shell crabs. The tomatoes' natural acidity cuts into the rich flavor of the crab, and the curry provides an intoxicatingly exotic note. For a final touch of whimsy, a cumin vinaigrette strewn with pine nuts, apple, and Belgian endive is spooned about the plate. Grilled shrimp or even chicken is an excellent substitute for the crab.

CURRIED TOMATO SAUCE

1 shallot, minced
2 cloves garlic, minced
1 tablespoon minced peeled fresh ginger
2 teaspoons minced lemongrass
2 tablespoons extra virgin olive oil
1 teaspoon spicy Madras curry powder
1 teaspoon sweet curry powder
4 small red tomatoes, diced
2 tablespoons chopped fresh cilantro
1 tablespoon white wine vinegar
½ cup water
Salt and freshly ground black pepper

SOFT-SHELL CRABS

2 tablespoons flour
¼ cup pine nuts, toasted and ground
Salt and freshly ground black pepper
1½ tablespoons grapeseed oil
4 soft-shell crabs, cleaned

CUMIN VINAIGRETTE

1 tablespoon cumin seeds, toasted and
  coarsely ground
1 tablespoon white wine vinegar
½ cup extra virgin olive oil
1 tablespoon chopped fresh chives
4 leaves Belgian endive, julienned
½ Granny Smith apple, julienned
3 tablespoons pine nuts, toasted
Salt and freshly ground pepper

GARNISH

4 teaspoons finely chiffonade-cut
  fresh cilantro

METHOD

To prepare the sauce: Sauté the shallot, garlic, ginger, and lemongrass in the olive oil over medium heat until translucent, about 5 minutes. Add the curry powders, tomatoes, cilantro, vinegar, and water; cook for 10 to 15 minutes, or until the tomatoes are tender and the flavors have melded. Season to taste with salt and pepper.

To prepare the crabs: Mix the flour and pine nuts together and season with salt and pepper. Heat the grapeseed oil in a sauté pan over medium-high heat. Dredge the soft-shell crabs in the flour mixture; add to the pan and sauté for 3 minutes on each side, or until golden brown. Remove from the pan and cut each crab in half; season with salt.

To prepare the vinaigrette: Just before serving, whisk the cumin and vinegar together, then slowly whisk in the olive oil. Warm the vinaigrette over medium heat until hot. Turn off the heat and add the chives, endive, apple, and pine nuts; season to taste with salt and pepper.

ASSEMBLY

Spoon some of the sauce and cumin vinaigrette onto each plate. Stand up 2 soft-shell crab halves in the center of each plate and spoon over more of the vinaigrette. Sprinkle with the cilantro.

WINE NOTES

The curried tomato sauce and the cumin vinaigrette pack a punch, so it is important that the wine choice favor the taste of the crab. An Austrian Gewürztraminer from Gross does the trick. This wine is lighter and more acrobatic than most of its flabby, slow-moving cousins from Alsace. All of the spice notes in the Gross work to tame the aggressive sauce, allowing the flavor of the soft-shells to shine.

Paella-Stuffed Heirloom Tomato

Serves 4

The sweet, meaty, slightly acidic tomato is an ideal foil for the lusty shellfish-flavored rice, and a saffron vinaigrette provides a sublime flavor complement to both of them. The ultimate beauty is that the tomato makes the paella more substantial without adding unnecessary richness.

PAELLA

¾ cup minced yellow onion
1 clove garlic, thinly sliced
1 teaspoon lightly crushed saffron threads
2 tablespoons extra virgin olive oil
1 cup short-grain Spanish rice
1 cup Chicken Stock (*see Appendices*)
1 cup clam juice
20 mussels, scrubbed clean
   and debearded
32 littleneck clams, scrubbed clean
1 cup shucked English peas
Salt

TOMATOES

4 large red tomatoes
4 cloves garlic
4 sprigs thyme
4 teaspoons extra virgin olive oil

SAFFRON VINAIGRETTE

Pinch of saffron
2 tablespoons minced shallot
½ cup clam juice
2 tablespoons white wine vinegar
½ cup extra virgin olive oil
Salt and freshly ground black pepper

GARNISH

4 teaspoons finely chiffonade-cut fresh
   flat-leaf parsley

METHOD

To prepare the paella: Sauté the onion, garlic, and saffron in the olive oil in a medium paella pan over medium heat for 5 minutes. Add the rice and cook until the rice is toasted, about 5 minutes. Add the stock and clam juice; simmer for 5 minutes. Arrange the mussels, clams, and peas over the rice and cover. Cook over medium-low heat for 30 to 45 minutes, or until the rice is al dente and the mussels and clams have opened. Discard any unopened clams or mussels. Season the paella with salt.

To prepare the tomatoes: Preheat the oven to 350°F. Blanch the tomatoes in boiling salted water for 1 minute to loosen the skin. Peel the skin from the bottom of the tomato to the top, leaving a small piece attached to the top of the tomato. Twist the ends of the tomato skin together on top of the tomato. Cut the tops off the tomatoes about 1 inch from the top. Carefully hollow out the inside of the tomatoes, keeping the tomatoes intact. Place a garlic clove and a thyme sprig inside each tomato and replace the tops. Place the tomatoes in an ovenproof pan and drizzle the olive oil over. Cook the tomatoes for 10 to 15 minutes, or until just softened.

To prepare the vinaigrette: Heat the saffron and shallot in the clam juice for 1 minute. Remove from the heat and whisk in the vinegar and olive oil. Season to taste with salt and pepper.

ASSEMBLY

Remove all but 8 mussels and 12 clams from their shells. Fill the tomatoes with some of the paella mixture and shelled mussels and clams. Balance the tomato tops over the stuffed tomatoes. Spoon a small mound of the paella mixture in the center of each plate and place a stuffed tomato atop the mound. Arrange the reserved mussels and clams in their shells around each tomato. Spoon the saffron vinaigrette over each tomato and around the plate and sprinkle with the parsley.

WINE NOTES

Bright, unoaked wines are the best match for the tomatoes and saffron in this dish. With its aromas of citrus and nectarines, Tim Adams Riesling from the Clare Valley in South Australia highlights the clean flavors of the shellfish. Fillaboa's Albariño from the Rias Baixas region of Spain is also a splendid combination with the saffron.

Open-Face White Anchovy and Tomato Tart with Caper Vinaigrette

Serves 4

*The great thing about this preparation is that it is easily customized to suit your needs.
It can be made any size, and the topping can be adjusted accordingly. Here, anchovies and tomatoes come together
in a heavenly pairing; a caper vinaigrette and a few herbs finish off the tart with
a playful touch. A small green salad on the side would make this a delightful summertime midday meal.*

TART CRUSTS

1 tablespoon minced garlic
¼ cup minced shallot
1 tablespoon extra virgin olive oil
1 cup (2 sticks) chilled butter, cubed
1 pound (3½ cups) all-purpose flour
8 ounces cream cheese
1 egg, beaten

TOPPING

3 cloves garlic, thinly sliced
1 shallot, julienned
1 tablespoon plus 2 teaspoons
   extra virgin olive oil
3 small red tomatoes, cored and cut
   into eighths
1 tablespoon tomato paste
2 tablespoons drained capers
2 cups yellow grape tomatoes, cut into
   thin rings
28 white anchovies

CAPER VINAIGRETTE

2 white anchovies, mashed
2 tablespoons drained capers, halved
⅓ cup extra virgin olive oil
1½ tablespoons freshly squeezed
   lemon juice

GARNISH

2 tablespoons chopped fresh
   flat-leaf parsley
Freshly ground black pepper

METHOD

To prepare the tart crusts: Sauté the garlic and shallot in the olive oil over medium heat for 2 minutes, or until translucent. Cool to room temperature. Place the butter, flour, and cream cheese in the bowl of an electric mixer, along with the cooled shallot mixture. Mix on medium speed with the paddle attachment for 5 minutes, or until all the ingredients come together and you can see streaks of cream cheese in the dough. Form the dough into a ball and wrap tightly in plastic wrap. Refrigerate the dough for 1 hour. Preheat the oven to 350°F. Roll out the dough into four 7-inch circles. Roll up the edges of the dough circles to create a slight rim and place on a sheet pan lined with parchment paper. Brush the circles with the beaten egg and bake for 12 to 15 minutes, or until golden brown. Cool the tart crusts slightly.

To prepare the topping and bake the tarts: Sauté the garlic and shallot in the 1 tablespoon olive oil over medium heat for 5 minutes. Add the red tomatoes, tomato paste, and capers; cook over medium-low heat until the liquid is cooked out of the tomatoes, about 10 minutes. Press 3 tablespoons of the mixture through a sieve. Whisk the 2 teaspoons olive oil into the sieved pulp and set aside for a garnish.

Preheat the oven to 400°F. Spread some of the red tomato mixture over the crusts and arrange the yellow tomato rings in a pinwheel shape on top. Arrange 7 of the anchovies over the tomatoes in a pinwheel shape on each tart (allow for some overhang with the anchovies, as they will shrink once heated). Bake the tarts for 12 minutes, or until warmed through.

To prepare the vinaigrette: Combine all of the ingredients and whisk together until incorporated.

ASSEMBLY

Place a tart in the center of each plate; sprinkle with the parsley and spoon the reserved tomato garnish around the plate. Drizzle the caper vinaigrette around the plate and top with pepper.

WINE NOTES

The acidic elements of this dish—the tomatoes and capers—are tempered by the buttery crust and the salty tang of the anchovies. A Marlborough, New Zealand, Sauvignon Blanc from Isabel is a stunning companion for these ingredients. The wine's intense aromatics and vibrant mouthfeel stand up to the tomatoes and capers without bowing to the richness of the tart shell. The gooseberry and tropical fruit notes of the Sauvignon Blanc add a further layer of complexity to the pairing.

Fresh Mozzarella–Covered Cherry Tomatoes with Rapini and Olive Oil–Poached Tomatoes

Serves 4

Incredible as a warm-weather appetizer, this may be the ultimate outdoor or picnic dish.
Tomatoes appear both raw, inside the mozzarella, and cooked, their flavor concentrated after slow poaching in olive oil.
Rapini provides an important contrast to the rich cheese and poached tomatoes. Chicken or fish
off the grill would be an inspired main course accompaniment, followed perhaps by a melon and berry salad.

OLIVE OIL–POACHED TOMATOES
6 plum tomatoes
2 cups extra virgin olive oil
1 sprig rosemary
Salt and freshly ground black pepper

BASIL VINAIGRETTE
1 clove garlic, smashed
8 leaves fresh basil
3 tablespoons balsamic vinegar
½ cup extra virgin olive oil
Salt and freshly ground black pepper

MOZZARELLA-COVERED TOMATOES
1 gallon water
¾ cup kosher salt
1 pound mozzarella cheese curd, cut into
  1-inch cubes
3 tablespoons chopped fresh basil
12 cherry tomatoes, peeled

RAPINI
2 tablespoons basil vinaigrette (above)
4 stalks rapini, blanched and cut into
  2-inch-long pieces
Salt and freshly ground black pepper

METHOD

To prepare the olive oil–poached tomatoes: Preheat the oven to 275°F. Remove the core from the tomatoes, leaving them whole. Place them standing upright in an ovenproof pan just large enough to hold them. Add the olive oil and rosemary and cover with aluminum foil. Bake for 3 to 4 hours, or until the skin easily comes off the tomatoes. Let cool. Remove the tomatoes from the oil and discard the skins and seeds. Strain the oil and refrigerate for another use. (The oil will have a pleasant tomato aroma.) Coarsely chop the tomato flesh and season with salt and pepper.

To prepare the basil vinaigrette: Place the garlic and basil in a mortar and smash with the pestle. Slowly work in the vinegar and olive oil until fully incorporated. Season to taste with salt and pepper.

To prepare the mozzarella-covered tomatoes: Cut twelve 4-inch-square sheets of plastic wrap and set aside. In a large pot, heat the water and kosher salt to 180°F. Place the cheese curd in a colander that will fit into the pot so that the curd is submerged. Submerge the colander in the water for 1 to 2 minutes, until the cubes of curd begin to stick together. Lift the colander out of the water, leaving the pot of water over the heat so that it maintains the 180°F temperature. Using a wooden spoon, knead the curd for 30 seconds, until it forms a mass with a stringy, taffylike consistency. If the curd seizes up because it is too cool, briefly submerge the colander in the hot water to make the curd pliable again; but be careful not to overwork the cheese or it will become tough.

Using your hands, pull off a small piece of curd (about a tablespoonful). Place it on one of the sheets of plastic wrap and sprinkle with a little of the basil. Pat the curd into a 3-inch circle ⅛ inch thick. Place a peeled tomato in the center of the cheese and completely enclose the tomato in the cheese. Wrap tightly in the plastic wrap, twisting to create a seal. Repeat this process with the remaining tomatoes and basil; in order to keep the cheese pliable, you will need to dip the colander back into the 180°F water for a few seconds before breaking off each piece of curd. Just prior to serving, remove the plastic wrap from the cheese-covered tomatoes and place them bottom side up on a sheet pan. Heat under the broiler for 2 to 3 minutes, or until the cheese is golden brown on top.

To prepare the rapini: Heat the vinaigrette in a sauté pan over medium heat. Add the rapini and cook for 2 minutes, or until the rapini is heated through. Add the olive oil-poached tomatoes and additional vinaigrette, if desired. Season to taste with salt and pepper.

TOMATOES

Fresh Mozzarella–Covered Cherry Tomatoes with
Rapini and Olive Oil–Poached Tomatoes

ASSEMBLY
Spoon some of the rapini mixture into the center of each plate and arrange 3 of the mozzarella-covered tomatoes over the rapini. Spoon some of the vinaigrette over the tomatoes.

WINE NOTES
Sicily is one of the most exciting up-and-coming wine regions in Italy. Many Sicilian winemakers are finding ways to blend tradition with technology and new grape varietals. Cusumano is one of the area's leaders, producing a blend of Insolia (a native variety) and Chardonnay to craft a medium-bodied wine called "Angimbé" that pairs magically with this dish. Unlike lighter-bodied wines that slash through the flavors of this dish, the Cusumano matches the weight of the mozzarella as well as the acidity of the tomatoes.

Kumamoto Oysters with Tomato Water Gelée

Serves 4

This first course makes a very elegant start for a special meal. Each oyster is contained in a cucumber gelée, which superbly cuts into the sweet, slightly briny taste of the bivalve. Tomato gelée, pickled radish, and grapefruit round out the dish with refreshing bursts of flavor and playful textural notes. These oyster gelées would also be a decadent garnish in a chilled tomato soup. To push this creation truly over the top, try garnishing the plate with generous dollops of caviar.

OYSTERS

3 cucumbers
6 sheets gelatin, bloomed
2 tablespoons freshly squeezed lime juice
12 Kumamoto oysters, shucked

TOMATO WATER GELÉE

1 cup Tomato Water *(see Appendices)*
2 sheets gelatin, bloomed
Freshly ground black pepper

PICKLED RED RADISHES

¼ cup water
⅓ cup sugar
½ cup rice wine vinegar
1 bay leaf
1 teaspoon yellow or brown mustard seeds
½ teaspoon fennel seeds
½ star anise
1 dried Thai chile
2 allspice berries
4 red radishes, cut into eighths

TOMATO VINAIGRETTE

1 small red tomato, puréed and passed
  through a fine-mesh sieve
1 teaspoon apple cider vinegar
1 teaspoon freshly squeezed lime juice
1 tablespoon extra virgin olive oil
Salt and freshly ground black pepper

GARNISH

¼ cup thin slices seeded, peeled,
  halved cucumber
8 yellow grapefruit segments, supremed
  and cut into sixths
½ cup quartered yellow teardrop tomatoes
1 teaspoon finely grated lemon zest
¼ cup micro cilantro sprouts (or chopped
  fresh cilantro)
Freshly ground black pepper
4 teaspoons freshly squeezed lime juice
4 teaspoons extra virgin olive oil

METHOD

To prepare the oysters: Cut the outer portion of 1 of the cucumbers into a brunoise, using the green skin and a little of the cucumber meat. Juice the remaining cucumbers in a juicer and pass through a fine-mesh sieve. Warm the cucumber juice slightly; remove from the heat and add the gelatin and lime juice. Line up 12 shot glasses and put 1 teaspoon of the cucumber brunoise in the bottom of each glass. Place an oyster on top of the cucumber in each glass and pour in enough cucumber juice mixture to just cover the oyster. Refrigerate overnight.

To prepare the tomato water gelée: Warm the Tomato Water slightly on the stove. Remove from the heat; stir in the gelatin and season with pepper. Pour the mixture into a small container and refrigerate overnight. Just prior to use, scrape the gelée with a fork to create small chunks.

To prepare the radishes: Combine all the ingredients in a saucepan and bring to a simmer. Cook for 3 minutes. Remove from the heat and refrigerate until needed. Drain the radishes just prior to use.

To prepare the tomato vinaigrette: Whisk together the tomato purée, vinegar, lime juice, and olive oil. Season to taste with salt and pepper.

ASSEMBLY

Dip the bottom of the shot glasses in hot water to loosen the gelée. Invert the cups onto a plate. Place 3 oyster gelées on each serving plate in a line. Spoon the tomato gelée and vinaigrette around the oysters. Scatter some of the cucumber slices, grapefruit, and teardrop tomatoes around the plate. Sprinkle the lemon zest and cilantro sprouts around the plate. Top with pepper and drizzle the lime juice and olive oil around the plate.

WINE NOTES

The salty flavor of the oysters, the high acidity from the pickled radishes, and the citrus notes from the grapefruit and lime all point to a Champagne pairing. Gaston Chiquet's "Tradition," a Champagne from Dizy, doesn't overpower the delicate, tantalizing elements of this dish.

CHEESE

Goat Cheese Cheesecake with Crispy Pepper Tuile and Sundried Tomato–Almond Vinaigrette

Serves 8

This delicate preparation works equally well as a dessert or an appetizer.
A tomato-almond vinaigrette, flecked with shredded arugula, provides just the right piquant flavor notes
to contrast with the creamy cheesecake. A peppery potato tuile adds a crispy texture and playful bite.
Best of all, perhaps, this cheesecake can be made ahead and served when needed.

TUILES

1 medium russet potato, roasted and riced
2 large egg whites
1 tablespoon butter, melted
1 tablespoon freshly ground black pepper
Salt

FILLING

8 ounces cream cheese, softened
8 ounces soft fresh goat cheese, softened
¼ cup sugar
2 large eggs
3 tablespoons freshly squeezed
   lemon juice
2 teaspoons salt
3 cups sour cream
½ cup crumbled soft fresh goat cheese
Freshly ground black pepper

CHEESECAKE CRUSTS

1 cup almonds, toasted and ground
¼ cup chopped sundried tomatoes
¼ cup cornmeal
1 teaspoon freshly ground black pepper
½ teaspoon salt
2 tablespoons butter, melted

SUNDRIED TOMATO–ALMOND VINAIGRETTE

1 cup extra virgin olive oil
2 tablespoons red wine vinegar
¼ cup chopped sundried tomatoes
½ cup almonds, toasted and chopped
2 tablespoons shredded arugula
Salt and freshly ground black pepper

METHOD

To prepare the tuiles: Preheat the oven to 225°F. Line a sheet pan with a Silpat or other nonstick silicone pan liner. Place the potato, egg whites, butter, and pepper in the bowl of an electric mixer and beat with the paddle attachment on medium speed for 2 to 3 minutes, or until smooth. Season with salt. Spread the tuile batter into 4-inch-long by 1½-inch-wide free-form strips on the prepared pan. Make extra tuiles, because they break easily. Bake the tuiles for 20 to 30 minutes, or until lightly golden brown. Remove from the Silpat with an offset spatula while still warm. Store in an airtight container until ready to use.

To prepare the filling: Place the cream cheese and softened goat cheese in the bowl of an electric mixer and whip with the paddle attachment on medium speed for 3 to 5 minutes. Add the sugar and eggs; mix until incorporated. Add the lemon juice, salt, and sour cream; mix until incorporated. Remove from the mixer and gently fold in the crumbled goat cheese. Season to taste with salt and pepper.

To prepare the crusts: Preheat the oven to 300°F. Process the almonds, tomatoes, cornmeal, pepper, salt, and butter in a food processor until combined. Butter the insides of four 3-inch-diameter by 1¾-inch-high ring molds and wrap the bottoms with aluminum foil, making sure the foil comes at least 1 inch up the outside of the mold. Place the prepared ring molds on a rimmed sheet pan. Firmly press the almond crust into the bottom of each mold.

To prepare the cheesecakes: Fill the ring molds with the cheesecake batter to ½ inch from the top. Add about ½ inch of water to the pan and bake for 40 to 50 minutes, or until the cheesecakes are just set. Cool the cheesecakes completely. Remove the foil and loosen the edges of the mold with a knife. Unmold the cheesecakes.

To prepare the vinaigrette: Whisk together the olive oil, vinegar, tomatoes, almonds, and arugula. Season to taste with salt and pepper.

ASSEMBLY

Place a cheesecake in the center of each plate and spoon the vinaigrette around the plate. Gently set a tuile in each cheesecake at an angle.

WINE NOTES

In terms of wine pairing, this course is like an awkward adolescent—it's not quite sweet enough for a dessert wine, but it's entirely unfit for a dry red or white wine. During the tasting, a Sherry—Domecq's "Sibarita" Palo Cortado—gloriously emerged as the perfect match. The amber-colored Sherry teems with aromas of spices and nuttiness that complement the almonds and the lightly peppery tuiles. Also, the high acid of the Palo Cortado melts into the goat cheese, lightening the overall weight of the cheesecake.

Crepes with Explorateur Cheese and Red Wine Dates

Serves 4

*Explorateur cheese is so creamy and rich it is almost like a pastry cream, especially if it has been slightly warmed.
Here the cheese is contained (barely) in meltingly soft crepes. A wine reduction strewn with
dried fruits and a buttery puréed almond sauce add complexity and depth of flavor. The crowning touch, though,
is the quenelle of delicately sweet dates, which integrates the other components with elegance.
These crepes will satisfy even those who do not crave cheese at the conclusion of a meal.*

DRIED FRUIT SAUCE
2 tablespoons sugar
2 teaspoons water
1 tablespoon butter
⅓ cup sliced almonds
1 tablespoon dried currants
1 tablespoon chopped dried sweet cherries
1 tablespoon chopped dried cranberries
½ cup Red Wine Reduction
 (see Appendices)
½ teaspoon freshly ground black pepper

RED WINE DATES
12 dates, pitted and chopped
½ cup Red Wine Reduction
 (see Appendices)
2 teaspoons chopped fresh rosemary

ALMOND SAUCE
½ cup almonds, soaked in water
 overnight and drained
½ cup water
1 tablespoon extra virgin olive oil
1 teaspoon sugar
Salt and freshly ground black pepper

CREPES
1¾ cups pastry flour
1 tablespoon sugar
½ teaspoon salt
2 cups milk
5 large eggs
5 tablespoons butter, melted
¼ cup butter, clarified
8 ounces Explorateur cheese, rind removed,
 cut into 8 equal pieces (3 by ½ by ¼ inch)

GARNISH
4 teaspoons extra virgin olive oil
1 tablespoon diagonally cut 1-inch
 pieces fresh chives
2 teaspoons fresh rosemary leaves
Freshly ground black pepper

METHOD
To prepare the dried fruit sauce: In a heavy-bottomed small sauté pan, combine the sugar and water; cook over medium heat without stirring for 5 to 8 minutes, or until golden brown. Swirl the pan as necessary to distribute the caramel. Add the butter and almonds and cook for 2 minutes, stirring to combine. Add the dried fruits, wine reduction, and pepper and stir to combine.

To prepare the dates: Place the dates, wine reduction, and rosemary in a saucepan; cook over medium-low heat for 5 minutes, or until the flavors have combined.

To prepare the almond sauce: Purée the almonds, water, olive oil, and sugar in a blender until smooth. Season to taste with salt and pepper. Warm over medium heat just prior to use.

To prepare the crepes: Preheat the oven to 350°F. Combine the flour, sugar, salt, milk, eggs, and melted butter in a mixing bowl with a whisk to mix thoroughly. Heat a crepe pan over medium-high heat and brush it with just enough of the clarified butter to coat the bottom of the pan. Using a measuring ladle, add 2 ounces of the batter to the pan and cook the crepe for 2 minutes, or until the edges begin to harden. Carefully flip the crepe over and cook for 30 seconds on the other side. Remove from the pan and lay the crepe flat on a sheet pan. Repeat with the clarified butter and crepe batter to make 8 crepes. Fill each crepe with 1 ounce of the cheese. Roll the crepes up and trim the edges. Just prior to serving, warm the crepes in the oven for 2 minutes.

ASSEMBLY
Spoon some of the almond sauce in the center of each plate. Place 2 crepes, one overlapping the other, atop the sauce. Place a quenelle-shaped piece of the date mixture in front of the crepes and spoon the dried fruit sauce around the plate. Drizzle the olive oil around the crepes and sprinkle with the chives and rosemary. Top with pepper.

WINE NOTES
Port is a seemingly logical choice with Explorateur cheese and dates, but both vintage and tawny versions overpower the crepes. A better answer is the Exceptional Reserve Riesling by Freie Weingartner from the Wachau region of Austria. The Exceptional Reserve—the equivalent of a German Auslese—has enough sweetness to dovetail with the dates while still allowing the pungent flavor of the cheese to shine.

Apple and Aged Cheddar Cheese Soufflé

Serves 4

*If there is a greater combination than apple and Cheddar cheese, I have yet to taste it.
This soufflé elevates two earthbound ingredients into the stratosphere of the sublime. A simple apple-pecan sauce
is all that is required to complete this dessert, which will end any special dinner on a truly profound note.*

APPLE-PECAN SAUCE

1 Granny Smith apple, peeled and cut into
  small dice
2 tablespoons butter
¼ cup sugar
1 teaspoon fresh thyme leaves
¼ cup chopped pecans
2 teaspoons balsamic vinegar

SOUFFLÉS

1 cup small-diced Granny Smith apples
2 teaspoons golden brown sugar
¼ teaspoon ground cinnamon
1 teaspoon chopped fresh rosemary
½ cup egg whites (from about 4 large eggs)
4 tablespoons plus 2 teaspoons butter
1 cup milk
⅔ cup flour
4 large egg yolks
6 ounces aged Cheddar cheese, grated

METHOD

To prepare the sauce: Sauté the apple with the butter and sugar over medium heat until caramelized, about 5 minutes. Stir in the thyme, pecans, and vinegar. Just prior to use, reheat if necessary.

To prepare the soufflés: Preheat the oven to 400°F. Toss the apples with the brown sugar, cinnamon, and rosemary and cook in a small saucepan over medium heat until the sugar has dissolved and the apples are tender, about 5 minutes. Remove from the heat and cool.

Butter and flour 4 individual soufflé dishes (about 3 inches in diameter and 3 inches high). In the bowl of an electric mixer fitted with the whisk attachment, whip the egg whites on medium speed to form stiff peaks, 3 to 4 minutes. Bring the butter and milk to a boil in a saucepan. Stir in the flour and bring to a second boil. Remove from the heat and stir in the egg yolks. Transfer to a large bowl and fold the whipped whites into the flour mixture in three additions. Fold three-fourths of the cheese into the soufflé batter.

Place a spoonful of the apple mixture in the bottom of each soufflé dish and fill to 1 inch from the top with soufflé batter. Place an additional spoonful of the apple mixture atop the soufflé mixture and sprinkle with the remaining cheese. Place the soufflé dishes in a roasting pan and add water to the pan to come halfway up the sides of the dishes. Bake for 35 minutes, or until the soufflés have risen and are golden brown. Loosen the sides of the soufflés with a knife; unmold the soufflés, then assemble and serve immediately.

ASSEMBLY

Place a soufflé in the center of each plate and spoon some of the warm apple-pecan sauce around the plate.

WINE NOTES

The light, airy soufflé has a touch of sweetness from the apple and requires a light- to medium-bodied wine that will not overwhelm its flavors. Aged Salon Champagne has the complexity and delicacy to provide the necessary balance. Salon—harvested entirely from the greatest Chardonnay vineyard in Champagne, Le Mesnil—lifts the flavor of the apple while absorbing the saltiness from the Cheddar in its tantalizing effervescence.

Maytag Blue Cheese and Apricot Tart with Sauternes Gelée

Serves 4

*Instead of a traditional cheese course before dessert, try this fairly simple tart.
The beautiful thing is that it can work nicely in just about any portion size, depending on the heartiness
of the other courses. You could even serve a wedge or two next to a mound of salad greens
for a splendid lunch. Or try presenting it with a whole roasted apricot on the side as a complete dessert.*

SAUTERNES GELÉE
325 ml (1½ cups) Sauternes
½ cup minced dried apricots
3 sheets gelatin, bloomed

THYME-BASIL SYRUP
½ cup Simple Syrup *(see Appendices)*
1 tablespoon fresh thyme
3 tablespoons fresh basil
½ teaspoon pink peppercorn shells

TART
10 ounces Cream Cheese Dough
  (see Appendices)
1 cup sliced shallots
1 tablespoon butter
1½ cups heavy whipping cream
2 large eggs
1 tablespoon fresh thyme
1 tablespoon chopped fresh parsley
Salt and freshly ground black pepper
½ cup julienned dried apricots
1½ cups crumbled Maytag blue cheese
6 tablespoons chopped toasted
  black walnuts

GARNISH
2 tablespoons chopped toasted
  black walnuts
2 tablespoons chopped fresh
  flat-leaf parsley
Freshly ground black pepper

METHOD
To prepare the gelée: Line a 5-inch-square dish with plastic wrap. Simmer the wine in a saucepan over medium heat until reduced by half, about 15 minutes. Remove from the heat and add the apricots and gelatin. Stir until combined. Pour the wine mixture into the plastic-lined dish and refrigerate overnight. Once the gelatin is set, remove from the mold and cut into large dice just prior to use.

To prepare the syrup: Purée the syrup, thyme, and basil in a blender until smooth. Refrigerate overnight. Pass through a sieve lined with a coffee filter and add the peppercorn shells. Refrigerate until ready to use.

To prepare the tart: Preheat the oven to 350°F. Line a sheet pan with parchment paper. Roll out the dough on a lightly floured surface to a ⅛-inch thickness. Line a 10-inch tart ring with the dough and place on the parchment-lined pan. Refrigerate the dough until ready to use. Sauté the shallots in the butter over medium heat for 10 minutes, or until golden brown and caramelized. Reserve 2 tablespoons of the shallots for the garnish. Whisk together the cream, eggs, thyme, and parsley, and season with salt and pepper. Spread the caramelized shallots in the bottom of the prepared tart ring; sprinkle the apricots, blue cheese, and nuts over the shallots. Pour the cream mixture over the cheese and nuts. Bake the tart for 45 minutes, or until golden brown. Cool slightly before removing from the ring mold and cutting into 8 pieces.

ASSEMBLY
Place 2 pieces of the tart in the center of each plate. Sprinkle the reserved caramelized shallots and the walnuts around the tart. Place 6 or 7 pieces of the gelée around the tart and drizzle the syrup around the plate. Sprinkle with the chopped parsley and top with pepper.

WINE NOTES
My first memorable wine and food pairing was Roquefort cheese and Sauternes. The saltiness of the Roquefort matched with the sweet apricot flavors of Sauternes provides a brilliant contrast. The same magic occurs in this course between the Maytag tart and a Château Raymond-Lafon Sauternes. The addition of the Sauternes gelée to the dish further amplifies the combination.

DESSERTS

Chocolate Pudding Cake with Coconut Ice Cream

Serves 4

It's hard to beat the combination of chocolate and coconut, as this irresistible dessert definitively proves.
The intensely flavored pudding cake virtually disappears in your mouth, while the coconut ice cream provides a creamy
and cool counterpoint. For good measure, an ethereal coconut emulsion is spooned about the plate. Finally, strips
of crystallized ginger and slices of crispy toasted coquito nuts dropped on and around the cake offer whimsical textural notes.
Decadent? Perhaps. Heavenly? By all means.

COCONUT ICE CREAM

1 cup heavy whipping cream
1 cup unsweetened coconut milk
4 large egg yolks
¼ cup sugar
½ cup shredded coconut, toasted

PUDDING CAKE

1 cup flour
1½ cups golden brown sugar
½ cup unsweetened cocoa powder
2 teaspoons baking powder
1 cup heavy whipping cream
1¼ cups coconut water (not coconut milk)

COCONUT EMULSION

1 cup coconut milk
1 tablespoon sugar

GARNISH

2 tablespoons shredded coconut
¼ cup thinly sliced coquito nuts, toasted
2 tablespoons julienned crystallized ginger

METHOD

To prepare the ice cream: Prepare an ice water bath. Bring the cream and coconut milk to a boil in a medium saucepan. Whisk together the egg yolks and sugar in a bowl; slowly pour in some of the hot cream to temper the yolks. Pour the eggs into the cream mixture and cook over medium-low heat, stirring constantly, for 2 to 3 minutes, or until the custard coats the back of a spoon and steam rises from the top. Strain the custard through a fine-mesh sieve into a clean bowl and cool over the ice water bath, stirring occasionally, until the custard is chilled. Process the custard in an ice cream machine. Fold in the toasted coconut and keep the ice cream frozen until ready to use.

To prepare the pudding cake: Preheat the oven to 350°F. Line an 8-inch-square pan with plastic wrap. Whisk together the flour, ¾ cup of the brown sugar, ¼ cup of the cocoa powder, and the baking powder. Fold in the cream and pour the batter into the plastic-lined pan. Mix the remaining ¾ cup brown sugar and ¼ cup cocoa powder together and sprinkle over the top of the batter. Bring the coconut water to a boil and pour over the cake batter. Place the cake pan in a large roasting pan; pour enough water into the roasting pan to come 1 inch up the side of the cake pan. Bake the cake in the water bath for 50 minutes. Cool the cake to room temperature and invert it onto a sheet pan. Carefully pull away the plastic wrap. There should be a gooey puddinglike substance on the bottom of the cake. Using a 4-inch-diameter ring cutter, cut 4 portions from the cake. Clean the ring cutter before each cut.

To prepare the emulsion: Warm the coconut milk and sugar in a small saucepan. Just prior to use, froth with a handheld blender.

ASSEMBLY

Place a piece of the pudding cake in the center of each plate. Spoon the frothy portion of the emulsion around the pudding cakes. Place a quenelle-shaped scoop of the ice cream next to the cake and sprinkle the toasted coconut, coquito nuts, and crystallized ginger over the ice cream and around the cake.

WINE NOTES

The soft, nearly liquid texture of the pudding cake is similar to a flourless chocolate cake. The fifteen-year-old Bual Madeira from Cossart Gordon—a classic pairing with chocolate—has the acidity to cut through the rich cake, and its nuttiness boosts the flavor of the coconut ice cream.

Grilled Peach and Green Tea Custard Tart

Serves 4

At the height of their season, peaches in any form are heavenly, but in this dish they are truly sublime.
The flavors here are simultaneously straightforward and subtle. The nutty, delightfully crumbly tart crust embraces
the green tea custard and grilled peach slices. Thyme syrup and leaves lend a distinctive accent.
The beautiful thing is that this lovely, refined tart can be served either warm or at room temperature with equally
stunning results. Vanilla ice cream can be added if a richer course is desired.

THYME SYRUP
¼ cup loosely packed fresh thyme leaves
¼ cup blanched spinach leaves
½ cup Simple Syrup *(see Appendices)*

DOUGH
¼ cup (½ stick) butter, softened
1 cup powdered sugar
1½ teaspoons grated lemon zest
1 tablespoon grated orange zest
2 teaspoons ground cinnamon
1 teaspoon nutmeg
¼ teaspoon salt
1½ cups ground toasted, skinned hazelnuts
3 large egg yolks
1⅔ cups flour
1 teaspoon baking powder

GREEN TEA CUSTARD
2 cups heavy whipping cream
2 tablespoons green tea leaves, ground to a powder
3 large egg yolks
1 large egg
1½ cups sugar

PEACHES
3 peaches, peeled, halved, and pitted
1 tablespoon grapeseed oil

3 tablespoons chopped crystallized ginger

ORANGE-GINGER SAUCE
1 cup freshly squeezed orange juice
2 tablespoons julienned crystallized ginger

GARNISH
1 teaspoon fresh thyme leaves

METHOD

To prepare the syrup: Purée the thyme leaves, spinach, and syrup in a blender until smooth. Refrigerate overnight. Pass through a fine-mesh sieve and refrigerate until ready to use.

To prepare the dough: Cream the butter, powdered sugar, and lemon and orange zests together in the bowl of an electric mixer fitted with the paddle attachment on medium speed. Combine the cinnamon, nutmeg, salt, and hazelnuts in a bowl; add to the mixer and mix on medium speed until combined. Add the egg yolks and mix on medium speed until incorporated. Sift the flour and baking powder together; add to the mixer and mix on medium-low speed until incorporated. Form the dough into a ball; wrap it tightly in plastic wrap and refrigerate for 2 hours before rolling out. Roll out the dough on a lightly floured surface to a ⅛-inch thickness. Cut out four 4-inch-diameter circles and line four 3-inch-diameter by ½-inch-high tart rings with the dough. Refrigerate the prepared rings until ready to use.

To prepare the custard: Prepare an ice water bath. Place the cream and green tea in a large saucepan and bring to a simmer. Simmer for 2 minutes. Whisk together the egg yolks, egg, and sugar in a mixing bowl; slowly pour in some of the hot cream to temper the yolks. Pour the egg mixture into the cream and stir to combine. Divide the custard in half and cool half of the mixture over the ice water bath. Strain the other half of the custard through a fine-mesh sieve back into the saucepan and cook, stirring constantly, for 2 to 3 minutes, or until the custard coats the back of a spoon and steam rises from the top. Cool the cooked custard over the ice water bath, stirring occasionally, and reserve for the garnish.

To prepare the peaches: Prepare a medium-hot grill. Lightly brush the peaches with the oil and place over a moderate flame on the grill. Grill the peaches for 2 minutes, or until tender. Cut the grilled peach halves into ¼ inch-thick slices.

To prepare the tarts: Preheat the oven to 325°F. Place some of the chopped crystallized ginger in the bottom of each dough-lined tart ring. Spoon 1 tablespoonful of the custard into each. Arrange some of the peach slices in a pinwheel pattern in the tarts and cover with more of the green tea custard, allowing the peaches to peek through (reserve the remaining peach slices for the garnish). Bake the tarts for 20 to 25 minutes, or until the crust is golden brown.

To prepare the orange-ginger sauce: Place the orange juice in a small saucepan and bring to a simmer. Cook until reduced by two-thirds, then stir in the julienned crystallized ginger.

ASSEMBLY
Place a tart at 2 o'clock on each plate. Arrange some of the reserved peach slices at 7 o'clock. Spoon the reserved cooked green tea custard around the tart and peaches. Drizzle the thyme syrup and orange-ginger sauce around the plate. Sprinkle with the thyme leaves.

WINE NOTES
Alois Kracher crafts the greatest sweet wines in Austria and some of the finest in the world. The dried apricot and peach flavors of his 1998 Chardonnay Trockenbeerenauslese #2, from Neusiedlersee region, make it a magnificent pairing with the tart. The smoky, charred flavor of the grilled peaches is echoed in the oak aging the wine received.

Lemon Verbena Custard with Lace Cookies and Warm Berries

Serves 4

Though simple to prepare, this dessert can serve as an elegant conclusion for a special meal.
The fruit is enriched with a silky lemon verbena custard, and buttery, crispy lace cookies add a pleasant crunch.
Almost any fruit can be substituted for the berries: citrus, peaches, tropical fruits—whatever is in season.
And try substituting basil or mint for the lemon verbena; even a little white pepper would provide an interesting finishing touch.
In other words, don't hesitate to experiment.

LEMON VERBENA SYRUP
½ cup loosely packed fresh
   lemon verbena leaves
¼ cup fresh parsley, blanched
½ cup Simple Syrup *(see Appendices)*

CUSTARD
2¼ cups heavy whipping cream
½ cup loosely packed fresh
   lemon verbena leaves
15 large egg yolks
½ cup plus 1 tablespoon sugar

LACE COOKIES
1 cup almonds, finely ground
½ cup (1 stick) butter
½ cup sugar
½ cup corn syrup
½ cup plus 1½ tablespoons flour
½ teaspoon salt

BERRIES
½ cup fresh raspberries
½ cup fresh blackberries, halved
½ cup sliced fresh strawberries
¼ cup water
1 tablespoon freshly squeezed lemon juice

GARNISH
6 leaves fresh lemon verbena, finely
   chiffonade-cut

METHOD
To prepare the syrup: Purée the lemon verbena, parsley, and syrup in a blender until smooth. Refrigerate overnight. Pass through a fine-mesh sieve before using.

To prepare the custard: Prepare an ice water bath. Place the cream and lemon verbena in a saucepan and bring to a simmer. Simmer for 2 minutes, then strain out the lemon verbena. Whisk together the egg yolks and sugar in a bowl; slowly pour in some of the hot cream to temper the yolks. Pour the egg mixture and the cream into a double boiler set over simmering water. Cook, whisking occasionally, for 40 minutes, or until custardlike and thick. Cool over the ice water bath and refrigerate until ready to use.

To prepare the lace cookies: Preheat the oven to 350°F. Line a sheet pan with a Silpat or other nonstick silicone pan liner. Place the ground almonds, butter, and sugar in the bowl of an electric mixer and whip with the paddle attachment on medium speed until combined, about 2 minutes. Add the corn syrup and mix on medium speed until incorporated, about 1 minute. Stir in the flour and salt on low speed, about 2 minutes. Refrigerate the dough for 1 hour before using. Roll 1 heaping teaspoon of the dough into a ball and place on the Silpat-lined pan. Repeat with the remaining dough to make at least 12 cookies; it is good to make a few extra in case of breakage. Place the balls 2 inches apart. Bake for 10 minutes, or until golden brown and crispy. If desired, cut the cookies while they are still hot with a ring cutter for a perfectly round shape.

To prepare the berries: Warm all the berries, the water, and the lemon juice in a saucepan over low heat for 2 to 3 minutes, or until the juices are just beginning to be released from the berries.

ASSEMBLY
Place a cookie in the center of each plate and top with 1 tablespoonful of the custard. Spoon a few of the berries over the custard and top with another cookie. Place another tablespoonful of the custard atop the cookie and spoon more berries over the custard. Top with a final cookie. Drizzle a few more berries and the juices from the berries around the plate. Spoon the syrup around the plate and sprinkle with the lemon verbena chiffonade.

WINE NOTES
The fresh berries and the lemon verbena custard have delicate flavors that would be crushed by a fat, syrupy dessert wine. Saracco's Moscato d'Asti, best consumed young, has a light effervescence and just a touch of sweetness. The tantalizing, fruity flavor of the Moscato supports the berry notes of the dish and lifts the flavor in the custard.

Melon Gelées with Honeydew Melon Soup
Serves 4

In a veritable celebration of melon, three distinctive and refreshing gelées containing honeydew and red and yellow watermelon sit elegantly in a pool of soothing honeydew soup. Pieces of cantaloupe are strewn about, while wisps of mint, a touch of Basil Oil, and a grind of black pepper provide enticing aromatic notes. This dish is very light but explosive in flavor; it could work as a fun transitional dessert course or, if desired, as a stunning finale.

MELON GELÉES

1 cup small-diced red watermelon
1 cup small-diced yellow watermelon
1 cup small-diced honeydew melon
1 cantaloupe, chopped
½ cup Simple Syrup *(see Appendices)*
1 lime, juiced
8 sheets gelatin, bloomed

SOUP

1 honeydew melon, chopped
1 tablespoon freshly squeezed lemon juice
¼ cup loosely packed fresh mint leaves

GARNISH

½ cup small-diced cantaloupe
4 teaspoons Basil Oil *(see Appendices)*
¼ cup loosely packed finely shredded
  fresh basil
Freshly ground black pepper

METHOD

To prepare the gelées: Line up 12 shot glasses or sake cups and fill 4 halfway with the diced red watermelon; fill 4 halfway with the diced yellow watermelon; fill the remaining 4 halfway with the diced honeydew. Purée the chopped cantaloupe, syrup, and lime juice in a blender until smooth and pass through a fine-mesh sieve. Place the cantaloupe purée in a small saucepan and add the bloomed gelatin. Warm over medium heat for 2 minutes. Pour the liquid into the prepared shot glasses, just covering the fruit. Refrigerate overnight.

To prepare the soup: Purée the honeydew, lemon juice, and mint in a blender and pass through a fine-mesh sieve. Chill until ready to use.

ASSEMBLY

Unmold 1 of each type of fruit gelée and arrange in the center of a shallow bowl. (If necessary, dip the bottom of the shot glass in warm water to loosen the gelée.) Repeat with the remaining gelées and bowls. Sprinkle the diced cantaloupe around the bowl. Pour some of the honeydew soup around the gelées and drizzle the Basil Oil around the soup. Sprinkle with the shredded basil and top with pepper.

WINE NOTES

This dish is especially refreshing, and the accompanying wine should not detract from that character. Rivetti "La Spinetta" Moscato d'Asti is a semisparkling, semisweet wine from the Piedmont. Its light body and attractive, fruity aroma and flavor are wonderful with the delicate honeydew melon soup and the melon gelées.

Banana and White Chocolate Bread Pudding with Bittersweet Chocolate–Marshmallow Ice Cream

Serves 4

If you are looking for a finale that is comforting and sinful, this is surely it. There is nothing restrained or subtle about this bread pudding—just straightforward indulgence. The marriage of banana, chocolate, and marshmallow has near-universal appeal, and the result here is over-the-top. If you really want to stop the show, substitute bittersweet chocolate for the white chocolate in the bread pudding; your guests will be rendered speechless!

MARSHMALLOWS

1 cup sugar
1 cup corn syrup
1 vanilla bean, pulp scraped
   and reserved
2 large egg whites
10 sheets gelatin, bloomed
¼ cup cornstarch
¼ cup powdered sugar

BITTERSWEET CHOCOLATE–MARSHMALLOW ICE CREAM

1½ cups heavy whipping cream
½ cup milk
4 large egg yolks
¼ cup sugar
4 ounces bittersweet chocolate, chopped
2 cups ½-inch-dice marshmallows (above)

BANANA BREAD

1 cup (2 sticks) butter, softened
1½ cups golden brown sugar
4 large eggs
4 cups flour
2 teaspoons baking soda
1 teaspoon salt
1½ cups mashed overripe bananas
2 tablespoons freshly squeezed
   lemon juice
1 teaspoon vanilla extract

BREAD PUDDING

3 cups heavy whipping cream
2 large eggs
4 large egg yolks
½ cup sugar
Diced banana bread (above)
10 ounces white chocolate, chopped
3 cups ¾-inch-dice marshmallows (above)

METHOD

To prepare the marshmallows: Line a sheet pan with plastic wrap and oil the plastic lightly. Place the sugar, corn syrup, and vanilla pulp in a small saucepan and stir over medium-low heat until it reaches the soft ball stage (234°-240°F). In the meantime, in the bowl of an electric mixer fitted with the whip attachment, whip the egg whites on medium speed to soft peaks, 2 to 3 minutes. When the syrup mixture reaches the soft ball stage, add the gelatin. While beating the egg whites on low, slowly pour in the syrup mixture, being careful not to splatter the syrup, mixing for 2 minutes. Once all the syrup is added, increase the speed to high and whip until shiny and glossy, about 5 minutes. Pour onto the plastic-lined sheet pan and let set at room temperature for about 3 hours. Combine the cornstarch and powdered sugar; lightly dust the marshmallow sheet with the mixture. Cut enough marshmallows in a ½-inch dice to measure 2 cups and cut the remainder in a ¾-inch dice.

To prepare the ice cream: Prepare an ice water bath. Bring the cream and milk to a boil in a medium saucepan. Whisk together the egg yolks and sugar in a bowl; slowly pour in some of the hot cream to temper the yolks. Pour the eggs into the cream mixture and cook over medium-low heat, stirring constantly, for 2 to 3 minutes, or until the custard coats the back of a spoon and steam rises from the top. Place the chocolate in another bowl. Strain the custard through a fine-mesh sieve into the chocolate and whisk until the chocolate is completely melted. Cool over the ice water bath, stirring occasionally, until the custard is chilled. Process the custard in an ice cream machine. Fold in the marshmallows and keep the ice cream frozen until ready to use.

To prepare the banana bread: Preheat the oven to 350˚F. Line a large loaf pan with parchment paper. Place the butter and brown sugar in the bowl of an electric mixer and cream with the paddle attachment on medium speed until light and fluffy, about 3 minutes. Add the eggs one at a time, mixing on medium-low speed until incorporated after each addition, 1 minute each time. Sift the flour, baking soda, and salt together; add to the bowl and mix on medium-low speed until combined, 2 to 3 minutes. Toss together the bananas, lemon juice, and vanilla in another mixing bowl. Fold the banana mixture into the batter. Pour the batter into the parchment-lined loaf pan and bake for 45 minutes to 1 hour, or until golden brown and firm to the touch. Cool and cut into ¾-inch dice.

To prepare the bread pudding: Preheat the oven to 350˚F. Line an 8-inch-square pan with parchment paper. In a large mixing bowl, whisk together the cream, eggs, egg yolks, and sugar until combined. Add the diced banana bread, white chocolate, and marshmallows; fold together until combined. Pour the pudding into the parchment-lined pan and bake for 1 hour and 15 minutes, or until golden brown.

Banana and White Chocolate Bread Pudding with Bittersweet Chocolate–Marshmallow Ice Cream

HAZELNUT PRALINE
½ cup sugar
¼ cup water
½ cup hazelnuts, toasted and
  skins removed

CARAMEL-VINEGAR SAUCE
½ cup sugar
¼ cup plus 1 tablespoon water
3 tablespoons rice wine vinegar

To prepare the praline: Lightly oil a nonstick sheet pan or line it with a Silpat or other nonstick silicone pan liner. In a heavy-bottomed medium sauté pan, combine the sugar and water; cook over medium heat without stirring for 5 to 8 minutes, or until golden brown. Swirl the pan as necessary to distribute the caramel. Stir in the nuts. If any of the sugar crystallizes, continue to cook over low heat to remelt. Pour the nut mixture onto the prepared pan. Let cool and then chop coarsely. (For individual "pralined" nuts, remove the nuts from the caramel individually with a fork and set them on a sheet pan to cool.) Store the praline in an airtight container at room temperature until ready to use.

To prepare the caramel sauce: In a heavy-bottomed small sauté pan, combine the sugar and water; cook over medium heat without stirring for 5 to 8 minutes, or until golden brown. Swirl the pan as necessary to distribute the caramel. Remove from the heat, add the vinegar, and mix thoroughly. Allow the sauce to cool slightly before using.

ASSEMBLY
Cut four 3-inch squares of the bread pudding and place a piece in the center of each plate. Spoon the caramel sauce around the bread pudding. Sprinkle the hazelnut praline around the plate and place a quenelle-shaped scoop of the ice cream atop the bread pudding.

WINE NOTES
One of the classic rules in pairing wine with dessert is that the wine must be sweeter than the food. Because of the power and sweetness of the bread pudding, this consideration must be borne in mind. Emilio Lustau's Deluxe Cream Sherry "Capataz Andres" has the stuffing and round, unctuous texture to pair with this dessert. The long, nutty finish of the Lustau also highlights the flavor of the hazelnut praline.

Carrot Cake with Crème Fraîche Frosting and Pecan–Brown Butter Sauce

Serves 4

Carrot cake is a perennial favorite, but with the addition of currants this version is especially delightful. A pecan brown butter sauce provides a note of nutty, buttery richness. For an interesting variation, try substituting parsnips for the carrots; serve it without explanation, and your guests won't believe they're eating parsnips for dessert!

BUTTERMILK ICE CREAM
1 cup heavy whipping cream
1 cup buttermilk
5 large egg yolks
½ cup sugar

CARROT CAKE
1 cup (2 sticks) butter, melted
1 cup sugar
2 large eggs
1 cup bread flour
½ teaspoon salt
½ teaspoon baking soda
1 teaspoon ground cinnamon
2 cups grated carrot
½ cup chopped pecans, toasted
½ cup dried currants

FROSTING
⅓ cup sugar
5 ounces cream cheese, softened
6 tablespoons cubed butter, softened
⅔ cup crème fraîche
½ vanilla bean, pulp scraped
   and reserved
1 teaspoon freshly squeezed lemon juice

CARROT SAUCE
1 cup chopped carrots
1 cup water
½ cup Simple Syrup *(see Appendices)*
½ vanilla bean, pulp scraped and reserved

CARROT STRIPS
1 carrot, peeled
1 cup Simple Syrup *(see Appendices)*

PECAN–BROWN BUTTER SAUCE
¼ cup (½ stick) butter
1 tablespoon sugar
2 tablespoons finely ground pecans

METHOD

To prepare the ice cream: Prepare an ice water bath. Bring the cream and buttermilk to a boil in a large saucepan. Whisk together the egg yolks and sugar in a bowl; slowly pour in some of the hot cream to temper the yolks. Pour the eggs into the cream mixture and cook over medium-low heat, stirring constantly, for 2 to 3 minutes, or until the custard coats the back of a spoon and steam rises from the top. Strain the custard through a fine-mesh sieve and cool over the ice water bath, stirring occasionally, until the custard is chilled. Process the custard in an ice cream machine and freeze until ready to use.

To prepare the cake: Preheat the oven to 350°F. Butter a 6-inch ring mold and place it on a sheet tray lined with parchment paper. In the bowl of an electric mixer fitted with the paddle attachment, cream the butter and sugar on medium speed, about 3 minutes. Add the eggs and beat for 2 minutes. Sift together the flour, salt, baking soda, and cinnamon. Add the dry ingredients to the creamed mixture and mix on medium-low speed for 3 minutes, or until incorporated. Stir in the carrot, pecans, and currants. Pour the batter into the ring mold and bake for 35 minutes, or until the cake springs back when touched in the center. Cool the cake and remove from the mold. Slice the cake in half horizontally.

To prepare the frosting and frost the cake: Place the sugar, cream cheese, butter, crème fraîche, vanilla pulp, and lemon juice in the bowl of an electric mixer and whip with the whisk attachment on medium-high speed until smooth, 3 to 5 minutes. Spread some of the frosting over 1 carrot cake half; top with the second layer and frost the top and sides with the remaining frosting. Refrigerate the cake for 1 hour before cutting into 4 pieces.

To prepare the carrot sauce: Combine the carrots, water, syrup, and vanilla pulp in a saucepan; bring to a simmer. Cook over medium heat until the carrots are tender, 10 to 15 minutes. Purée in a blender and pass though a fine-mesh sieve.

To prepare the carrot strips: Using a vegetable peeler, peel long strips from the carrot. Place the strips and syrup in a saucepan and simmer over low heat for 5 to 7 minutes, or until the strips are tender but not fully cooked. Cool the strips in the syrup until ready to use.

To prepare the pecan-brown butter sauce: Melt the butter over medium-low heat, skimming away the milk solids that rise to the top. Once the butter has a nutty aroma, add the sugar and cook until the sugar has dissolved. Add the pecans and set aside until ready to use.

ASSEMBLY
Place a slice of the cake off center on each plate. Place a little mound of carrot strips opposite the cake and set a quenelle-shaped scoop of the ice cream atop the carrot strips. Spoon the carrot and pecan-brown butter sauces around the plate.

WINE NOTES
The crème fraîche frosting adds a layer of richness to the spice-filled carrot cake. The appropriate wine supplements these spices while providing a bright level of acidity to lighten the weight of the dessert. Isole e Olena's Vin Santo accomplishes both, its dried fruit and nutty character perfectly matching the currants mixed throughout the cake.

Honey Mascarpone Cannoli
with Candied Pine Nuts and Blueberries

Serves 4

*Although these cannoli are sinfully rich, they are not cloyingly sweet. A barely sweetened,
whipped mascarpone cream, lightly flavored with mint, is a delicious filling for the crispy, delicate cannoli shells.
A barely cooked blueberry sauce counterbalances the creamy mascarpone filling, and some crunchy candied
pine nuts provide textural contrast. All the components can be made well ahead of time for easy last-minute assembly.
For variations, fold dried fruits into the mascarpone cream, or use tropical fruits in place of the blueberries.*

CANNOLI

1 cup powdered sugar
½ cup egg whites (from about 4
   large eggs)
¾ cup (4½ ounces) pastry flour, sifted
½ cup (1 stick) butter, melted and cooled
   to room temperature

FILLING

¼ cup heavy whipping cream
¼ cup honey
2 cups mascarpone cheese, softened
¼ cup loosely packed chopped fresh mint
1 tablespoon lemon zest

CANDIED PINE NUTS

2 tablespoons sugar
1 tablespoon honey
½ cup pine nuts

MASCARPONE SAUCE

½ cup Simple Syrup *(see Appendices)*
½ cup packed fresh mint leaves
¼ cup mascarpone cheese
3 tablespoons heavy whipping cream
1 tablespoon freshly squeezed lemon juice

BLUEBERRIES

1½ cups fresh blueberries
2 tablespoons freshly squeezed
   lemon juice
2 tablespoons honey
2 tablespoons sugar

METHOD

To prepare the cannoli: Preheat the oven to 325°F. Line a sheet pan with a Silpat or other nonstick silicone pan liner. In the bowl of an electric mixer fitted with the whisk attachment, whip the sugar and egg whites on medium speed to form stiff peaks, 3 to 4 minutes. Fold in the flour in three additions. Fold in the melted butter until just incorporated. Thinly spread the batter into 5-inch circles on the prepared pan. Make at least 8 circles; it is good to have a few extra on hand in case of breakage. Bake the shells for 6 to 7 minutes, or until golden brown. Loosen the shells with an inverted spatula and immediately wrap around a 1½-inch-diameter dowel rod to form the cannoli shells. Remove from the rod and let cool completely. Store the shells in an airtight container until ready to use.

To prepare the filling: In the bowl of an electric mixer fitted with the whisk attachment, whip the cream and honey on medium speed to stiff peaks, 3 to 4 minutes. Fold in the mascarpone, mint, and lemon zest. Refrigerate until ready to use.

To prepare the pine nuts: Lightly oil a nonstick sheet pan or line it with a Silpat or other nonstick silicone pan liner. In a heavy-bottomed small saucepan, combine the sugar and honey; cook over medium heat without stirring for 5 to 8 minutes, or until golden brown. Swirl the pan as necessary to distribute the caramel. Stir in the nuts. Spread the mixture on the prepared pan and allow to harden at room temperature. Break up into small pieces.

To prepare the mascarpone sauce: Purée the syrup and mint leaves in a blender until smooth. Place 2 tablespoons of the mint syrup in a mixing bowl; reserve the remaining mint syrup for the garnish. Add the mascarpone, cream, and lemon juice to the mixing bowl and whisk the sauce until smooth.

To prepare the blueberries: Place the blueberries, lemon juice, honey, and sugar in a saucepan; cook over medium-low heat until all the flavors come together (don't stir much, to keep the blueberries whole). Remove from the heat and refrigerate until ready to use.

ASSEMBLY

Place the filling in a piping bag and fill each shell. Place some of the candied pine nuts at each end. Spoon some of the mascarpone sauce in the center of each plate and spoon some of the blueberries in the center of the sauce. Set 2 cannoli atop the blueberries and spoon some of the mint syrup around the plate. Sprinkle the remaining candied pine nuts around the plate.

WINE NOTES

It would be a disappointing pairing if the wine hid the bright, high-toned mint flavors and the understated honey in the mascarpone cannoli. A Bonnezeaux from René Renou, especially one with bottle age, is filled with honey and vanilla notes. This wine reinforces the mascarpone and the cannoli shell without disturbing the wonderful flavor of mint.

Chocolate Terrine with Cherries and Burnt Orange Cream

Serves 8

This terrine is surprisingly simple to prepare, but the results are extraordinary. Succulent sweet cherry pieces are suspended in silky-smooth ganache, which is exquisitely wrapped in the candied rind of oranges. A dollop of burnt orange cream sits in the center of the plate with chopped pistachio praline strewn about. All the textures and flavors weave marvelously together. When you need a special dessert to end an important dinner, this won't let you down.

PRESERVED ORANGE STRIPS

3 oranges
2 cups Simple Syrup *(see Appendices)*

CHOCOLATE TERRINE

1 cup heavy whipping cream
9 ounces bittersweet chocolate, chopped
1 tablespoon sugar
1 tablespoon butter
Preserved orange strips (above)
12 Rainier cherries, pitted and halved
12 Bing cherries, pitted and halved

CANDIED ORANGE WRAP

10 oranges
3 cups Simple Syrup *(see Appendices)*

RAINIER CHERRY SAUCE

½ cup Rainier cherries, pitted
  and chopped
2 tablespoons water

BING CHERRY SAUCE

½ cup Bing cherries, pitted and chopped
2 tablespoons water

Continued

METHOD

To prepare the preserved orange strips: Cut off the rind from the oranges and reserve the rind. (Save the fruit for another use.) Cut the rind into ¼-inch-thick strips; place in a saucepan and add enough water to cover. Bring to a boil, then drain off the water. Repeat the boiling and draining three times. Cover the rind in the syrup and bring to a slow simmer; cook for 20 minutes. Drain the orange strips.

To prepare the terrine: Line an 8 by 1½ by 2¼-inch terrine mold with plastic wrap, allowing the wrap to hang over the outside of the mold. Bring the cream to a boil. Place the chocolate, sugar, and butter in a mixing bowl and pour the hot cream over. Whisk together until smooth. Add the preserved orange strips and all the cherries; fold gently together. Pour the mixture into the prepared mold; the mixture should fill the mold. Cover with the overhanging plastic wrap and refrigerate overnight.

To prepare the orange wrap: Peel the rind from the oranges using a vegetable peeler, making strips as wide as possible. Trim away any white pith still attached to the rinds. (Save the fruit for another use.) Place the rinds in a saucepan and add enough water to cover. Bring to a simmer (do not boil) and drain. Repeat the simmering and draining three times. Cover the rinds in the syrup in a saucepan and simmer slowly for 10 minutes. Drain the rinds. Lay a large piece of plastic wrap on a flat surface. Lay the orange rind pieces on the plastic wrap, outer side down and overlapping slightly, until they cover a 9 by 8-inch surface. Cover with a second piece of plastic wrap and press flat, then remove the second piece of plastic.

To wrap the terrine: Carefully unmold the terrine and remove the plastic wrap. Invert the terrine onto the bottom edge of the orange wrap. Wrap the orange wrap around the terrine, and then wrap the whole terrine tightly in plastic wrap to help keep its form. Return to the refrigerator and chill until ready to use.

To prepare the Rainier cherry sauce: Place the cherries and water in a small saucepan and bring to a simmer. Pass though a fine-mesh sieve, pressing with a spoon to force out as much pulp as possible.

To prepare the Bing cherry sauce: Place the cherries and water in a small saucepan and bring to a simmer. Pass though a fine-mesh sieve, pressing with a spoon to force out as much pulp as possible.

DESSERTS

Chocolate Terrine with Cherries and Burnt Orange Cream

PISTACHIO PRALINE
½ cup sugar
¼ cup water
½ cup unsalted pistachios, shelled and
  skins removed

BURNT ORANGE CREAM
2 cups freshly squeezed orange juice
½ cup sugar
1 cup heavy whipping cream
1 cup mascarpone cheese

GARNISH
¼ cup diced Bing cherries
¼ cup diced Rainier cherries

To prepare the praline: Lightly oil a nonstick sheet pan or line it with a Silpat or other nonstick silicone pan liner. In a heavy-bottomed medium sauté pan, combine the sugar and water; cook over medium heat without stirring for 5 to 8 minutes, or until golden brown. Swirl the pan as necessary to distribute the caramel. Stir in the nuts. If any of the sugar crystallizes, continue to cook over low heat to remelt. Pour the nut mixture onto the prepared pan. Let cool and then chop coarsely. (For individual "pralined" nuts, remove the nuts from the caramel individually with a fork and set them on a sheet pan to cool.) Store the praline in an airtight container at room temperature until ready to use.

To prepare the cream: Combine the orange juice and sugar in a saucepan and bring to a simmer. Simmer until it is reduced to ¼ cup, 20 to 25 minutes. (The flavor will be very intense.) Chill the orange reduction. Place the cream and mascarpone in the bowl of an electric mixer and using the whisk attachment on medium speed, whip until stiff, 2 to 3 minutes. Fold in the chilled orange reduction and refrigerate until ready to use.

ASSEMBLY
Spoon the Rainier cherry and Bing cherry sauces around each plate in an abstract pattern. Leaving the plastic wrap on the terrine, cut eight ½-inch-thick slices from the terrine, cleaning the knife between each cut. Peel off the plastic wrap and place a slice of the terrine on each plate on an angle at 10 o'clock. Place a quenelle-shaped scoop of the burnt orange cream next to the terrine. Scatter some of the diced cherries around the plate. Sprinkle the pistachio praline over the cream and around the plate.

WINE NOTES
Bodegas Olivares makes a unique late-harvest wine in Jumilla, Spain, from the red Monastrell, or Mourvèdre, grape. The wine has a wealth of coffee and chocolate aromas, as well as notes of black cherry and plum. There is a moderate level of tannin in the Olivares, which is unusual for dessert wines but is outstanding with the chocolate terrine. The dark, rich chocolate is cut by the tannin, while the flavor of cherry in the wine is complemented by the cherries on the plate.

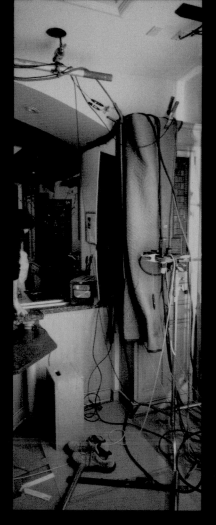

APPENDICES

Basil Oil

Yield: 1 cup

½ cup firmly packed fresh basil
½ cup firmly packed spinach leaves
¼ cup firmly packed fresh flat-leaf parsley
¼ cup extra virgin olive oil
1 cup grapeseed oil

METHOD Blanch the basil, spinach, and parsley in boiling salted water for 45 seconds. Immediately shock in ice water and drain. Chop the mixture coarsely and squeeze out the excess water. Purée in a blender with the olive and grapeseed oils for 3 to 4 minutes, or until bright green. Pour into a container, cover, and refrigerate for 1 day.

Strain the oil through a fine-mesh sieve and discard the solids. Refrigerate for 1 day, decant, and refrigerate until ready to use, or up to 2 weeks.

Beef Stock

Yield: about 2 quarts

6 pounds beef bones
1 tablespoon grapeseed oil
2 cups chopped carrots
2 cups chopped celery
4 cups chopped yellow onions
3 cloves garlic
½ cup chopped tomatoes
2 cups red wine
1 bay leaf
1 tablespoon whole black
   peppercorns

METHOD Preheat the oven to 450°F. Place the bones in a roasting pan and roast for 1 hour, or until golden brown; turn the bones after 30 minutes to ensure even browning. Transfer the bones to a large stockpot. Place the roasting pan on the stove top over medium-high heat and add the grapeseed oil, carrots, celery, onions, and garlic to the pan. Cook until the vegetables are caramelized, 10 to 15 minutes. Add the tomatoes and cook for 2 minutes. Deglaze the pan with the wine and cook until most of the wine has been absorbed. Transfer the vegetables and any remaining liquid to the stockpot. Add the bay leaf, peppercorns, and enough cold water to cover. Bring to a boil; decrease the heat to low and simmer slowly for 6 to 8 hours, periodically skimming the impurities that rise to the surface. Strain through a fine-mesh sieve. Store in the refrigerator up to 4 days, or freeze up to 2 months.

Braised Artichokes

Yield: 8 artichoke bottoms with stems

2 cups chopped carrots
2 cups chopped celery
2 cups chopped yellow onions
¼ cup grapeseed oil
8 raw artichoke bottoms with
    stems attached
2 lemons, cut in half
½ cup butter
4 bay leaves

METHOD In a large saucepan, cook the carrots, celery, and onions in the grapeseed oil over medium-high heat until caramelized, 10 to 15 minutes. Add the artichokes, lemon, and enough water to cover; bring to a simmer. Add the butter and bay leaves and cover with a piece of parchment paper cut to fit inside the pan, directly on top of the artichokes. Decrease the heat to low and cook the artichokes for 30 to 40 minutes, or until just tender. A knife should slide into the artichokes easily, but with slight resistance. Remove the artichokes from the liquid and discard the vegetables and cooking liquid. Scrape out the chokes, and refrigerate until needed.

Braised Collard Greens

Yield: 2 cups

½ cup chopped uncooked bacon
4 cups chopped collard greens
1 tablespoon sugar
2 tablespoons red wine vinegar
1 cup water
Salt and freshly ground black pepper

METHOD Render the fat from the bacon in a medium sauté pan over medium heat, about 3 minutes. Add the collard greens and cook for 3 minutes. Add the sugar, vinegar, and water; decrease the heat to low and continue to cook for 30 to 45 minutes, or until the greens are tender. Season to taste with salt and pepper.

Chicken Stock

Yield: 2 quarts

6 pounds chicken bones
3 cups chopped yellow onions
2 cups chopped carrots
2 cups chopped celery
1 cup chopped leeks
1 tablespoon whole white peppercorns
1 bay leaf

METHOD Place all of the ingredients in a large stockpot and add enough cold water to just cover. Bring to a boil; decrease the heat to low and simmer slowly for 4 hours, skimming every 30 minutes to remove impurities that rise to the surface. Strain through a fine-mesh sieve into another pot; discard the solids. Simmer over medium heat for 30 to 45 minutes, or until reduced to 2 quarts. Store in the refrigerator up to 4 days, or freeze up to 2 months.

Cilantro Oil

Yield: 1/2 cup

1/2 cup firmly packed fresh cilantro
1/4 cup firmly packed fresh flat-leaf parsley
1/2 cup grapeseed oil
1/4 cup extra virgin olive oil

METHOD Sauté the cilantro and parsley in 1 tablespoon of the grapeseed oil over medium heat for 2 minutes, or until wilted. Immediately shock in ice water and drain. Chop the mixture coarsely and squeeze out the excess water. Purée in a blender with the remaining grapeseed oil and the olive oil for 3 to 4 minutes, or until bright green. Pour into a container, cover, and refrigerate for 1 day.

Strain the oil through a fine-mesh sieve and discard the solids. Refrigerate for 1 day, decant, and refrigerate until ready to use, or up to 2 weeks.

Corn Water

Yield: 3 cups

10 ears sweet corn, husks removed
1 yellow onion, chopped
2 bay leaves

METHOD Cut the corn kernels from the cobs. Place the cobs and kernels, with the onion and bay leaves, in a medium stockpot. Add enough cold water to cover the cobs and kernels by 2 inches and bring to a slow simmer. Simmer for 1 hour, then strain through a fine-mesh sieve. Transfer to a saucepan and simmer over medium-low heat until reduced to 3 cups, about 20 minutes. Store in the refrigerator up to 4 days, or freeze up to 2 months.

Cream Cheese Dough

Yield: 1¹/₂ pounds dough

8 ounces chilled cream cheese,
  cut into chunks
8 ounces chilled butter, cut into chunks
8 ounces all-purpose flour

METHOD In the bowl of an electric mixer fitted with the paddle attachment, combine the cream cheese, butter, and flour on medium speed until the dough just comes together, about 5 minutes (there should still be streaks of cream cheese). Remove the dough from the bowl, pat into a disk, cover with plastic wrap, and refrigerate for at least 1 hour before use.

Duck Confit

Yield: 4 legs and thighs

6 tablespoons kosher salt
1 tablespoon sugar
1 tablespoon coarsely ground black pepper
2 tablespoons sliced garlic
2 teaspoons chopped fresh ginger
4 duck legs with thighs attached
2½ cups duck fat

METHOD Combine the salt, sugar, pepper, garlic, and ginger in a small bowl. Rub the duck legs with the mixture, pack tightly in a small container, and cover with plastic wrap. Refrigerate for 24 hours, turning the pieces over after 12 hours.

Preheat the oven to 225°F. Rinse the duck legs and place in a heavy-bottomed pot. Add the duck fat and cover the pot. Bake for 6 hours, or until the meat is fork-tender. Cool the duck in the fat and store in the refrigerator up to 2 weeks.

Fennel Oil

Yield: ½ cup

½ cup firmly packed fresh fennel fronds
½ cup firmly packed spinach leaves
½ cup firmly packed fresh flat-leaf parsley
¼ cup extra virgin olive oil
¾ cup grapeseed oil

METHOD Blanch the fennel fronds, spinach, and parsley in boiling salted water for 45 seconds. Immediately shock in ice water and drain. Chop the mixture coarsely and squeeze out the excess water. Purée in a blender with the olive and grapeseed oils for 3 to 4 minutes, or until bright green. Pour into a container, cover, and refrigerate for 1 day.

Strain the oil through a fine-mesh sieve and discard the solids. Refrigerate for 1 day, decant, and refrigerate until ready to use, or up to 2 weeks.

Fennel Stock

Yield: 2 quarts

4 large fennel bulbs with tops, chopped
1 yellow onion, chopped
2 bay leaves
1 teaspoon whole black peppercorns
4 quarts water

METHOD Place all the ingredients in a stockpot and bring to a boil. Decrease the heat to low and simmer for 1 hour. Strain the mixture through a fine-mesh sieve into another pot; discard the solids. Simmer over medium heat for 30 to 45 minutes, or until reduced to 2 quarts. Store in the refrigerator up to 4 days, or freeze up to 2 months.

Herb Oil

Yield: ¹/₂ cup

¼ cup firmly packed chopped fresh chives
¼ cup firmly packed fresh flat-leaf parsley
¼ cup firmly packed watercress leaves
½ cup grapeseed oil
¼ cup extra virgin olive oil

METHOD Sauté the chives, parsley, and watercress in 1 tablespoon of the grapeseed oil over medium heat for 2 minutes, or until wilted. Immediately shock in ice water and drain. Chop the mixture coarsely and squeeze out the excess water. Purée in a blender with the remaining grapeseed oil and the olive oil for 3 to 4 minutes, or until bright green. Pour into a container, cover, and refrigerate for 1 day.

Strain the oil through a fine-mesh sieve and discard the solids. Refrigerate for 1 day, decant, and refrigerate until ready to use, or up to 2 weeks.

Lamb Stock

Yield: about 2 quarts

6 pounds lamb bones
1 tablespoon grapeseed oil
2 cups chopped carrots
2 cups chopped celery
4 cups chopped yellow onions
3 cloves garlic
½ cup chopped tomatoes
2 cups red wine
1 bay leaf
1 tablespoon whole black peppercorns

METHOD Preheat the oven to 450°F. Place the bones in a roasting pan and roast for 1 hour, or until golden brown; turn the bones after 30 minutes to ensure even browning. Transfer the bones to a large stockpot. Place the roasting pan on the stove top over medium-high heat and add the grapeseed oil, carrots, celery, onions, and garlic to the pan. Cook until the vegetables are caramelized, 10 to 15 minutes. Add the tomatoes and cook for 2 minutes. Deglaze the pan with the wine and cook until most of the wine has been absorbed. Transfer the vegetables and any remaining liquid to the stockpot. Add the bay leaf, peppercorns, and enough cold water to cover. Bring to a boil; decrease the heat to low and simmer slowly for 6 to 8 hours, periodically skimming the impurities that rise to the surface. Strain through a fine-mesh sieve. Store in the refrigerator up to 4 days, or freeze up to 2 months.

Meat Stock Reduction

Yield: 1½ cups

2 cups chopped yellow onions
1 cup chopped carrots
1 cup chopped celery
2 tablespoons grapeseed oil
1 cup red wine
2 quarts Beef Stock (page 190)
4 sprigs thyme

METHOD Sauté the onions, carrots, and celery in the grapeseed oil in a medium saucepan over high heat for 10 minutes, or until golden brown and caramelized. Deglaze the pan with the wine and cook until most of the wine has been absorbed. Add the stock and simmer over low heat for 1 hour. Strain and return the liquid to the saucepan. Add the thyme and simmer for 5 minutes. Remove the thyme and simmer for about 30 minutes, or until reduced to 1½ cups. Strain through a fine-mesh sieve. Store in the refrigerator up to 4 days, or freeze up to 2 months.

Pickled Red Onion

Yield: about 1 cup

1 small red onion, julienned
½ cup water
½ cup rice wine vinegar
¼ cup sugar
1 tablespoon kosher salt
1 whole clove
1 teaspoon mustard seeds
1 teaspoon whole black peppercorns
1 teaspoon chopped fresh ginger

METHOD Combine all of the ingredients in a small saucepan and simmer over low heat for 5 minutes, or until the salt and sugar dissolve. Remove from the heat and let steep for 20 minutes. Refrigerate until ready to use.

Pickling Brine

Yield: 2 cups

1 cup water
½ cup rice wine vinegar
½ cup plus 2 tablespoons sugar
2 tablespoons kosher salt
1 whole clove
1 teaspoon mustard seeds
1 teaspoon whole black peppercorns
1 teaspoon chopped fresh ginger
½ jalapeño chile, seeded and chopped

METHOD Combine all of the ingredients in a small saucepan and simmer over low heat for 5 minutes, or until the salt and sugar dissolve. Let cool, strain out the solids, and use as needed.

Red Wine Reduction

Yield: 1 cup

1 cup chopped yellow onion
½ cup chopped carrot
1 leek (white part only), chopped
1 tablespoon grapeseed oil
1 Granny Smith apple, chopped
6 cups Merlot
3 cups Port

METHOD Sauté the onion, carrot, and leek in the grapeseed oil in a medium saucepan over high heat for 10 minutes, or until golden brown and caramelized. Add the apple, Merlot, and Port and simmer over medium heat for 1 hour. Strain through a fine-mesh sieve and return the liquid to the saucepan. Simmer for 30 to 40 minutes, or until reduced to 1 cup. Store in the refrigerator up to 4 days, or freeze up to 2 months.

Roasted Elephant Garlic

Yield: about 12 cloves

1 head elephant garlic, cloves peeled
3 cups milk
½ cup extra virgin olive oil

METHOD Preheat the oven to 350°F. Simmer the garlic cloves and milk in a small saucepan over low-medium heat for 10 minutes. Drain and discard the milk. Place the garlic cloves in a small ovenproof pan and add the olive oil. Cover with a tight-fitting lid or aluminum foil and bake for 45 to 60 minutes, or until the garlic cloves are soft. Store in the oil in the refrigerator for up to 2 weeks.

Roasted Garlic

Yield: about $^3/_4$ cup

4 heads garlic, tops cut off
3 cups milk
½ cup extra virgin olive oil

METHOD Preheat the oven to 350°F. Simmer the garlic heads and milk in a small saucepan over medium-low heat for 10 minutes. Drain and discard the milk. Place the garlic heads upright in a small ovenproof pan and add the olive oil. Cover with a tight-fitting lid or aluminum foil and bake for 1½ hours, or until the garlic heads are soft. Cool in the oil and then squeeze the cloves out of the skins. Store in the oil in the refrigerator for up to 2 weeks.

Roasted Wild Mushrooms

Yield: about 2 cups

8 cups assorted wild mushrooms
   (such as black trumpet, hedgehog,
   and stemmed shiitake)
1 cup chopped yellow onion
2 cloves garlic
2 sprigs thyme or rosemary
3 tablespoons extra virgin olive oil
1 cup water
Salt and freshly ground black pepper

METHOD Preheat the oven to 325°F. Place the mushrooms in an ovenproof pan and toss with the onion, garlic, thyme, and olive oil. Add the water and season with salt and pepper. Cover and bake for 30 to 40 minutes, or until the mushrooms are tender. Remove from the oven and cool in the cooking juices. Store in the refrigerator for up to 3 days.

Saffron Oil

Yield: 1/2 cup

1 teaspoon saffron threads, crushed
2 tablespoons water
2 tablespoons extra virgin olive oil
6 tablespoons grapeseed oil

METHOD Heat the saffron in a small sauté pan over low heat for 20 seconds to help release the oils present in the saffron. Add the water and quickly remove from the heat. Most of the water will immediately steam away. Using a rubber spatula, scrape the saffron and any remaining liquid into a blender. Add the olive and grapeseed oils; blend on high speed for 45 seconds, then refrigerate for 1 day. Unused oil can be stored in the refrigerator for several weeks.

Shellfish Oil

Yield: 3/4 cup

4 lobster heads
1 teaspoon tomato paste
1 cup grapeseed oil

METHOD Preheat the oven to 400°F. Place the lobster heads in a roasting pan and roast for 40 minutes, or until they are bright red. Break up the heads into small pieces and place in a small saucepan with the tomato paste and grapeseed oil. Heat the mixture over medium-low heat for 10 minutes, then cool and refrigerate for 2 days.

Strain the oil through a fine-mesh sieve lined with cheesecloth and discard the solids. Refrigerate until ready to use, or up to 2 weeks.

Shellfish Stock

Yield: 2 quarts

5 pounds lobster shells
½ cup chopped carrot
½ cup chopped celery
1 cup chopped leek
2 tablespoons canola oil
2 tablespoons tomato paste
1 cup red wine

METHOD Preheat the oven to 400°F. Roast the lobster shells in a roasting pan for 40 minutes, or until bright red and slightly golden brown.

In a large stockpot, cook the carrot, celery, and leek in the canola oil over medium-high heat for 10 minutes, or until golden brown and caramelized. Add the tomato paste and cook for 2 to 3 minutes. Deglaze the pan with the wine and cook for 3 minutes, or until most of the wine is absorbed. Add the lobster shells and enough cold water to cover by three-quarters. Simmer over low heat for 3 hours. Strain through a fine-mesh sieve into another pot; discard the solids. Simmer over low heat for 15 to 20 minutes, or until reduced to 2 quarts.

Simple Syrup

Yield: 2 ½ cups

1½ cups sugar
1½ cups water

METHOD Combine the sugar and water in a small saucepan. Bring to a boil, stirring frequently until all of the sugar is dissolved. Refrigerate until ready to use, or up to 1 month.

Tarragon Oil

Yield: ½ cup

½ cup firmly packed fresh tarragon
¼ cup firmly packed fresh flat-leaf parsley
½ cup grapeseed oil
¼ cup extra virgin olive oil

METHOD Sauté the tarragon and parsley in 1 tablespoon of the grapeseed oil over medium heat for 2 minutes, or until wilted. Immediately shock in ice water and drain. Chop the mixture coarsely and squeeze out the excess water. Purée in a blender with the remaining grapeseed oil and the olive oil for 3 to 4 minutes, or until bright green. Pour into a container, cover, and refrigerate for 1 day.

Strain the oil through a fine-mesh sieve and discard the solids. Refrigerate for 1 day, decant, and refrigerate until ready to use, or up to 2 weeks.

Tomato Confit

Yield: 1 cup

4 plum tomatoes
1 cup extra virgin olive oil
1 sprig rosemary

METHOD Preheat the oven to 275°F. Remove the core from the tomatoes, leaving them whole. Place them in an ovenproof pan just large enough to hold them. Add the olive oil and rosemary. Cover with aluminum foil and bake for 3 to 4 hours, or until the skin easily comes off the tomatoes. Let cool, remove from the oil, then remove the skins and seeds. Refrigerate the tomatoes until needed. Strain the oil; it will have a pleasant tomato aroma and can be used again.

Tomato Water

Yield: 1 1/2 to 2 cups

12 beefsteak tomatoes, chopped
1 tablespoon kosher salt

METHOD Blend the tomatoes and salt in a food processor. Tie up the purée in a large piece of cheesecloth and place the pouch in a colander set over a large bowl. Refrigerate for 8 hours, or until all the juices have dripped from the puréed tomatoes. Discard the solids and store the water in the refrigerator up to 4 days, or freeze up to 2 months.

Vegetable Stock

Yield: 2 quarts

1 cup chopped yellow onion
1 cup chopped carrots
1 cup chopped celery
1 cup chopped fennel bulb
1 red bell pepper, seeded and chopped
3 cloves garlic
1/2 cup chopped parsnip
1 bay leaf
1 teaspoon whole black peppercorns
4 quarts water

METHOD Place all the ingredients in a stockpot and bring to a boil. Reduce the heat to low and simmer for 1 hour. Strain the mixture through a fine-mesh sieve into another pot; discard the solids. Simmer over medium heat for 30 to 45 minutes, or until reduced to 2 quarts. Store in the refrigerator up to 4 days, or freeze up to 2 months.

BANANA FINGERLING POTATO
A light-skinned potato about the size of a large finger and curved like a banana. It has yellow flesh and a creamy texture.

BLOOMING
Dissolving or softening gelatin sheets in cool water. Blooming is done by placing the gelatin sheets in a bowl of cold water for 3 minutes, or until softened. Lift out the "bloomed" sheets and let any excess water drain off. If using powdered gelatin, follow the directions on the box, or sprinke ⅓ cup gelatin over a bowl of cold water and let sit for 2 minutes. Spoon out the bloomed gelatin and discard the soaking water.

BLUE HUBBARD SQUASH
A large winter squash about the size of a volleyball, with a bumpy outer skin that can range in color from light blue-gray to dark green. Its flesh is grainy and yellow-orange in color. Acorn squash can be a good flavor substitute.

BROCCOFLOWER
A bright chartreuse member of the cabbage family, broccoflower looks like a cross between broccoli and cauliflower but is a variety of the latter. It has tight florets and a mild flavor.

BRUNOISE-CUT
A very fine dice, approximately one-eighth-inch cubes.

CANDY CANE BEET
Also known as chioggia beets. The inside has concentric rings of red and white throughout.

CAPER BERRY
Pickled caper fruit that resembles a coarse green grape. It has a seedy, slightly starchy texture reminiscent of okra and a flavor similar to that of the caper bud but less intense.

CAUL FAT
The thin, lacy membrane of fat from the abdominal cavity lining of pigs or sheep. Pork caul fat is the most widely used and preferred. Your local butcher can order it, and it generally comes frozen.

CAULIFLOWER MUSHROOM
An off-white mushroom that resembles a cauliflower head in appearance but not in taste. It has a tender, spongy texture and a mild mushroom flavor.

CHIFFONADE-CUT
Fine strips about one-sixteenth of an inch wide. The term is usually used in reference to leafy vegetables or herbs that have been rolled up and sliced finely.

CHILE-GARLIC SAUCE
An Asian sauce that can be found in most supermarkets. It is made from dried crushed red pepper, garlic, vinegar, and sugar. There are many types and they vary in degrees of heat, so when using, select your personal preference of flavor and heat.

CHINESE BROCCOLI
Also known as Chinese kale or *gai lan.* It has green, waxy leaves, and the stems have a flowered top. The leaves, stems, and flowers are all used for cooking.

COCONUT WATER
The tasty, refreshing liquid inside a coconut. Look for young coconuts, which yield a greater quantity of liquid than older ones.

COQUITOS
Tiny dried coconuts about the size of a cherry. They are more intense in flavor than full-size coconuts.

ENOKI MUSHROOM
A white mushroom with a small cap and a very thin stem. Enokis come in clusters and are about four inches long, with tiny caps. To use, cut off the root end and retain the stem and cap. They can be cooked in a matter of seconds.

FIDDLEHEAD FERN
The young, tightly coiled frond of this fern is the edible part.

FISH SAUCE
A staple in Thai recipes, made from fermented fish and sea salt. It is used in place of salt in Thai cookery. There are many brands on the market, and selecting a good-quality fish sauce is essential. Look for sauces that have a clear reddish-brown color (like that of Scotch or whiskey), without any sediment present. If it is dark brown or muddy brown in color, it most likely is a low-grade fish sauce.

GELATIN SHEET
Commonly used in Europe, gelatin sheets are sold at some specialty foods shops in the United States. If unobtainable, substitute a teaspoon of powdered gelatin for each sheet of gelatin.

HAMACHI
Also known as yellowtail. This fish has a flavor and texture similar to tuna's, but it tastes more buttery and the flesh is creamy white.

HEDGEHOG MUSHROOM
A creamy yellow wild mushroom with a reddish-orange cap, slightly chewy texture, and mild flavor.

HIJIKI SEAWEED
A rich, chewy, full-flavored seaweed. It cannot be purchased fresh, but is readily available dried at Japanese and other Asian markets.

HOKKAIDO SQUASH
A small, round, bluish green squash with dry flesh of a dark orange color. Popular in Japan.

IVORY SALMON
A white-fleshed king salmon that is milder, silkier, and more buttery in flavor than its pink counterpart. Ivory salmon is hard to come by, but if you locate it, it is a treasure to savor.

JULIENNE-CUT
Strips (usually of vegetables) that are about one to two inches long and an eighth of an inch thick.

KAFFIR LIME LEAVES
The leaves of the kaffir lime tree are glossy and dark green and look like two leaves attached end to end. Once broken or chopped, they are incredibly aromatic, with floral and citrus notes. They are sold at Asian markets.

KUMAMOTO OYSTER
A sweet, plump, small oyster originally from Kumamoto Bay in Japan. Today they are farmed in Washington and California, and the best ones are from Humbolt Bay. Kumamoto oysters are sadly now extinct in Japan, but are thriving in the United States.

LANGOUSTINE
The French word for "prawn." Langoustines are generally six to eight inches in length and have a sweet, delicate flavor.

LEMON VERBENA
Sometimes called simply verbena. An easily grown herb with a pronounced lemon flavor. The leaves are long and narrow and have sawtooth edges.

MADRAS CURRY POWDER
A mixture of herbs and spices used in Indian cooking. The blend is mild in spice but full in flavor. It is generally made up from a blend of red chile, black pepper, fenugreek, coriander seeds, tumeric, cumin, mustard, and ginger.

MAHOGANY CLAM
A New England clam with a gray-purple shell. Mahogany clams average twenty-five per pound and are about the same size as Manila clams.

MARCONA ALMONDS
Sweet almonds from Marcona, Spain.

MICRO HERBS
Miniature herbs specially grown to have intense flavor yet remain tiny. If you cannot find micro herbs, their full-size counterparts, coarsely chopped or shredded, can be substituted.

RAPINI
Resembling a slim head of broccoli, rapini has a green slender stalk with small florets, jagged-edged leaves, and a bright green color. Also called broccoli rabe or raab.

RED KURI SQUASH
Also known as Baby Red Hubbard squash. A small skin-colored squash with red-orange flesh, its flavor is somewhat similar to that of a roasted chestnut. It is shaped like a top.

RICE BEANS
Small white beans that, when dried, are slightly larger than a cooked rice kernel. They have a delicate skin and sweet flavor.

SANSHO PEPPER
A very common seasoning in Japan. Sansho pepper is a relative of the Sichuan peppercorn. It has a soft lemon flavor and a delicate pepper bite and mild heat.

SUPREMED CITRUS
A citrus segment from which the white membrane and pith have been removed.

MIZUNA
A delicate dark green lettuce with a mild flavor similar in shape to a small oak leaf. Mizuna can often be found in supermarkets in the mesclun salad greens mix.

PANKO
Coarse Japanese breadcrumbs that are generally used on deep-fried foods to create an extra-crispy crust.

PEPITAS
The Spanish term for "pumpkin seeds." Look for dried raw seeds with their white hulls removed.

PINK PEPPERCORNS
The dried berries of a South American plant in the rose family. They have a loose pink shell that can be removed and used separately, if desired.

RAINIER CHERRY
A sweet cherry with creamy yellow flesh and red-blushed yellow skin. Available from June to early August.

RAMP
A wild onion that resembles a baby leek with broad leaves.

TOBIKO WASABI
Wasabi-flavored flying fish roe. The roe is chartreuse in color.

TATSOI
A tender salad green with small round leaves and a mild flavor.

TEMPERING
The process of slowly adding hot cream to eggs while whisking. This step keeps the eggs from scrambling when added to hot cream in making custard or ice cream.

TRUMPET ROYAL MUSHROOM
Also called a royal trumpet mushroom, it is light brown-gray in color with a trumpet-shaped cap. It has a delicate mushroom flavor and a tender texture when cooked.

YUZU CITRON
A Japanese citrus fruit about the size of a tangerine that is most commonly used for its aromatic rind. The juice is made by pressing the whole fruit—rind and pulp. It is sold at Japanese markets.

INDEX

INDEX

TEN SPEED PRESS

Box 7123
Berkeley, California 94707
www.tenspeed.com

Distributed in Australia by Simon & Schuster Australia, in Canada by Ten Speed
Press Canada, in New Zealand by Southern Publishers Group, in South Africa
by Real Books, and in the United Kingdom and Europe by Airlift Book Company.

Editors: Windy Ferges and Aaron Wehner
Research, development, and recipe testing: Sari Zernich, Charlie Trotter's
Copyeditor: H. Abigail Bok
Proofreader: Jasmine Star
Indexer: Ken DellaPenta
Design: Tim Bruce, LOWERCASE, INC.

Library of Congress Cataloging-in-Publication Data on file with publisher
Printed in Hong Kong
ISBN 1-58008-613-6
First printing, 2004

1 2 3 4 5 6 7 8 9 10 — 08 07 06 05 04

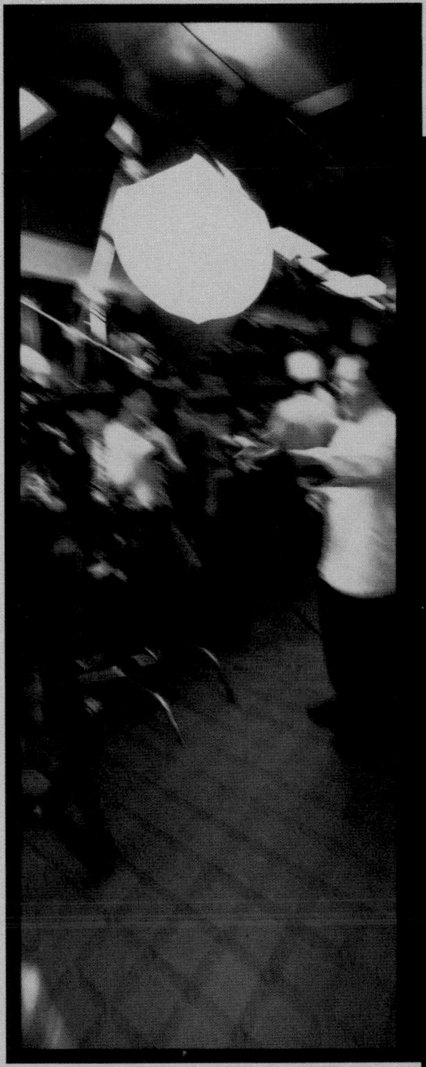
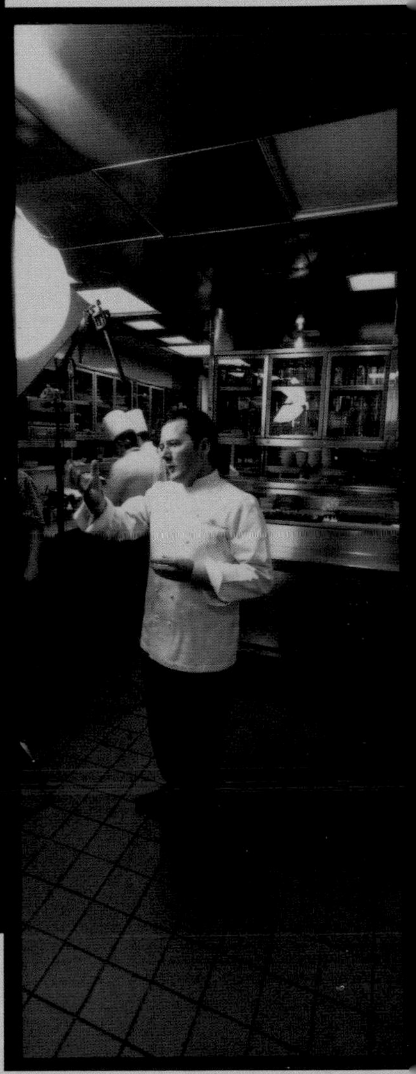